THAT JOKE ISN'T FUNNY ANYMORE

On the Death and Rebirth of Comedy

LOU PEREZ

BOMBARDIER

Published by Bombardier Books
An Imprint of Post Hill Press
ISBN: 978-1-63758-245-9
ISBN (eBook): 978-1-63758-246-6

That Joke Isn't Funny Anymore:
On the Death and Rebirth of Comedy
© 2022 by Lou Perez
All Rights Reserved

Cover design by Tiffani Shea
Interior Design by Yoni Limor
Cover image by Paul Rondeau

BOMBARDIER
BOOKS

Post Hill Press
New York • Nashville
posthillpress.com

Published in the United States of America
1 2 3 4 5 6 7 8 9 10

If we sometimes looked more inwardly, and employed the time in probing ourselves that we spend in examining others and learning about things exterior to us, we should easily discover how much our own fabric is built of failing and fragile pieces.

—Michel de Montaigne

Live

Laugh

Love

—Bessie Anderson Stanley (sort of)

For my sons, Andreas and Mateo

TABLE OF CONTENTS

1

A BRIEF HISTORY OF
THE DEATH OF COMEDY

I shouldn't have told anybody I was writing a book. There's already the stress of meeting deadlines—I haven't met *any* yet and already I'm asking my publisher for extensions. And every other day a well-meaning friend checks in and humiliates me with the question, "How is the book going?"

I don't know, man. But I hope by the end of it I do.

What makes matters worse is that I'm writing about comedy. You would think that would be fun—but those same friends have taken my subject as an open invitation to send me every awful thing that bears some resemblance to comedy today.

No one sends me funny shit anymore. Just links to the latest cringe from establishment shows like *Saturday Night Live*, *The Late Show with Stephen Colbert*, and whatever the hell Peacock is.

"Hey, Lou, have you seen this clip from the *Sex and the City* spinoff with the queer, nonbinary, bisexual stand-up comic?"

To think I almost got away with *not seeing* that clip of "Che Diaz" from *And Just Like That*!

I wanted to change my phone number—so my friends would stop texting me the link to it.

They tell me—and I don't mean *they* as in fictional Che's pronoun—that "comedy is dead." Well, if that's all you're watching it sure does look it.

I don't want to give you the wrong idea. This book is not meant to be comedy's obituary. But, if it were, we would have to talk about the year 2016. That's when I first recognized we might have a problem.

After Donald J. Trump won the presidential election concerned citizens—at least in the "press" over at *Paste* and *Vulture* magazines—began asking the all-important existential question: What would the role of comedy be under a President Trump?

Neither online magazine asked me—they asked people way more successful than I am.

But had they asked me, I would have said: "I don't know—what the fuck was the role of comedy under President Obama?"

As Rory Albanese, a former executive producer at *The Daily Show* and *The Nightly Show with Larry Wilmore*, told *Vulture*, "Comedy's role under Trump should be the same as it's always been: a heady mix of truth to power and fart jokes."

I like that message. After all, what comedian doesn't love the smell of his own fart jokes?

But when it comes to "truth to power," I don't remember comedians speaking much truth to power when that power was President Obama. Not even one fart joke at the expense of the 44th Commander-in-Chief. (I smell coverup.) Maybe comedians were so exhausted from eight years of George W. Bush punch lines that they needed two terms of Obama for rest and recovery.

If we're at least speaking truth to each other, regardless of our respective powers, what the original question about the role of comedy under Trump implied is that comedy *needed to be different* under Trump.

Now, did that mean comedians would no longer be cheerleaders for the executive branch—at least for the next four years—that is, until a Democrat was back in the White House?

Or were comedians and comedy journalists saying that we ought to get back to that whole speaking-truth-to-power thing from now on—no matter who's in power?

Two of the lowest points in comedy I can remember both went down on *Saturday Night Live*. Do you recall back in 2016 when the universe, in an act of incalculable cruelty, killed Leonard Cohen *and* Hillary Clinton's dream of becoming president of the United States in the same week?

SNL's response to that synchronicity was to have cast member Kate McKinnon dress up as Hillary Clinton, an impersonation she had regularly done before, to sing Leonard Cohen's masterpiece "Hallelujah."[1]

Hillary's white power suit was now a funeral garb and there were no punch lines in McKinnon's performance—just grieving over the Donald Trump presidency to come. Instead of speaking truth to power, *SNL* was mourning the peaceful transfer of power.

---

1   John Lennon's "Imagine" might be the only song that's been reprised more. Dearest celebrities, whatever your next cause du jour might be: Stop. Singing. These. Songs. There has to be another song you can "raise awareness" with!

The sorrow continued when President Obama vacated the Oval Office, and Cecily Strong and Sasheer Zamata sang "To Sir, with Love" to him.

If you don't get the reference, that's because it's from 1967. *To Sir, with Love* is a film starring the beloved Sidney Poitier.

Poitier plays a man, Mark Thackery, who is waiting to hear back about an engineering gig and passes the time teaching asshole high school kids in England to respect him and themselves. Spoiler: In the end he gets the engineering job—but decides to stay at the high school to teach more limey punks who don't deserve him or self-respect.

See, the metaphor is quite clear: Barack Obama was just like Mr. Thackery. And We the People were like those asshole English teenagers with Beatles haircuts. We didn't deserve Him. Unfortunately, Obama didn't stay to teach us. He would have—*I just know it!*—if it hadn't been for that damn 22nd Amendment and its presidential term limits!

Instead, our beloved prez went on to produce for Netflix—which is something to be thankful for. Because whenever you or the cast of season forty-two of *Saturday Night Live* misses Obama, you can just turn on the children's series *Waffles + Mochi*, where Hope still lives.[2]

If you look back at the years 2008–2016 you may justify the lack of jokes about Obama with, "Well, it's not like there was anything about the man you could make fun of."

But to believe that—to believe the man was a mic drop personified!—you would also have to be in the camp that thinks those eight years were also scandal free.

On August 28, 2021, Andrew Weinstein, Chair of the Democratic National Committee's Lawyers Council and an Obama White House appointee (as per his Twitter bio),

---

2   It is a very cute show. Former First Lady Michelle Obama is great in it. I wonder what actresses she beat out for the role.

tweeted, "Happy anniversary to the biggest scandal of the Obama presidency" with a picture of President Obama wearing the infamous tan suit.

Do you remember *The* Tan Suit? His supporters sure like to bring it up a lot.

Now I wish that suit was the biggest scandal of O's presidency. But unfortunately, I remember the Obama administration spying on Americans, prosecuting whistleblowers, the assassination of at least one US citizen, and Operation Fast and Furious—which was not part of the Vin Diesel/ Paul Walker canon. If I was able to forget that stuff and only remember the tan suit, I would.

I would also like to forget that time President Obama continued US involvement in Libya without congressional approval. I don't know if you can buy tan suits in Libya today, but you can buy tan slaves. I think that one deserves a legit *Thanks, Obama.*

I admit that I voted for President Obama in 2008, so I bear some responsibility for his foreign policy (but only up through 2012—because I voted for Gary Johnson that year[3]). I guess it's easier to overlook Obama's failings—or "scandals"—because the man has incredible charisma. It's off the charts. When he speaks he's almost messianic.

When Congress passed Obamacare, I thought Obama was literally going to be my doctor. In my fantasy, Doc Barack not only heals me but he also forgives my sins—and he does it all without charging a co-pay!

You know you've got charisma when you can spend eight years bombing countries—expanding the US's global footprint in the name of the War on Terror—and all some

---

3   I voted for Johnson again in 2016 and soon learned that my voting third-party in New York was somehow responsible for Trump winning. I had no idea third parties had no power and all the power simultaneously.

people remember (or, could it be, want others to remember?) is…that Tan Suit.

I remember when President Obama bombed that wedding party in Yemen. To be fair: No bride in Yemen wants Donald Trump or Joe Biden bombing her wedding. No bride anywhere on the planet wants that! But Barack Obama?

That's pretty cool. *That* is charisma. President Obama couldn't be there in person—but he did send a gift. *Not doing so* would have been a scandal.

While comedians were giving President Obama a pass, the president was making jokes of his own. At the 2010 White House Correspondents' Association Dinner, the most powerful man in the world roasted the Jonas Brothers who were in attendance.

"Sasha and Malia are huge fans," President Obama said. "But, boys, don't get any ideas. Two words for you: predator drones. You will never see it coming."

Obama has great comedic timing—his later work on *Between Two Ferns with Zach Galifianakis, Key & Peele,* and *Comedians in Cars Getting Coffee* with Jerry Seinfeld is awesome—but I didn't like the joke.[4]

Well, I didn't like that the president was telling it. Let's just say ordering death from the sky feels a lot like "punching down."

To be fair: I didn't like President George W. Bush's joke six years earlier at the Radio and Television Correspondents' Association. If you don't remember it, Dubya's bit was accompanied by a slide show. Over one photograph of him bending over in the Oval Office, looking through his legs, Bush says, "Those weapons of mass destruction gotta be somewhere."

---

4   Snow. Flake.

Later, over another photo, "Nope. No weapons over there." And the third beat of the joke: "Maybe under here."

Almost twenty years removed from that joke, I almost forgot about Bush's scandals. Forgive me. Since then he's slipped Michelle Obama pieces of candy a couple times at official ceremonies and done oil paintings of soldiers wounded under his command. As far as I can tell no WMDs have appeared in any of those portraits. "Nope. No weapons over there."

If we lived in an alternate reality where the biggest scandal of the Obama presidency was his tan suit—or putting Dijon mustard on a cheeseburger, as Sean Hannity and other right-wingers reported back in 2009—then I could understand the lack of Obama jokes…a little.

But as nice as that scandal-free fantasy would have been to live through—and a way less bloody one too—I didn't live through that. And, as an adult and a comedian, to pretend otherwise, and not crack jokes about it—now that would be a scandal.

* * *

I started doing political comedy toward the end of Obama's second term. Although I made jokes about the president, I never thought I was "speaking truth to power." I was just doing what I thought comedians were supposed to do: find the funny and go with it. I was ready to continue doing just that for our first madam president….

Then Trump won.

How. Did. That. Happen? Well, many theories were advanced: Hillary had not done her legwork in Wisconsin and Michigan. Russia had overrun Facebook with Pro-Trump ads.[5]

---

5   Which Facebook ad made you vote for Trump?

One thing is clear, after eight "scandal-less" years of Obama, the truth-to-power proponents finally had a president they were allowed to speak "truth" to—without worrying about being publicly shamed—and they let fly, emptying everything on the Big Orange Man Bad.

If you felt dangerous and brave making fun of Trump, you are delusional. I know "speaking truth to power" sounds like some warrior shit. But if you're doing it in the United States it doesn't take much bravery. Especially when it's against the correct targets.

As a comedian, I admit the plus side of telling yourself that you're speaking truth to power is that if a joke doesn't work you can just blame it on the truth.

Too much truth. Not enough room for a punch line.

"But part of me hopes Trump makes comedy illegal," Rory Albanese told *Vulture* in the lead-up to Trump's inauguration, "because I want to get in on the ground floor of the comedy speakeasy business. Gonna start bootleggin' jokes across state lines."[6]

No, Trump did not make comedy illegal. Even though he had good reason to try. He was universally hated by the powers that be in entertainment, academia, and politics and was a perpetual target of their mockery. You would think a thin-skinned, vindictive, and petty man—a fascist!—like Trump would have at least put James Corden before a firing squad. But no. Not here. Not in America.

I'm reminded of the brave Egyptian comedian Bassem Youssef, the "Jon Stewart of Egypt," who was forced to flee

---

6   The comedy speakeasy meme actually gained more traction for comedians who were right-of-center—or to be more accurate, comedians who went to bed moderates or even left-of-center and woke up to find themselves labeled right-wing or worse. Speakeasies are for the canceled. Goofing on Trump was not, is not, and will never be a cancellable offense.

his country for being, well, "the Jon Stewart of Egypt." Youssef's criticism of the Morsi regime eventually led him to seek refuge in the United States, meanwhile Jon Stewart who was wept over for leaving *The Daily Show*...his exile was self-chosen.

In Afghanistan the Taliban murdered TikTok comedian Nazar Mohammad (stage name: Khasha Zwan). Now I was no fan of Zwan. The guy was a fucking hack. The Taliban called him "obscene"—and I agree with that wholeheartedly—but that was no justification for his murder.

I'm not saying if you don't risk imprisonment or death for telling jokes that you have nothing to complain about. Germany prosecutes a comedian for making fun of Turkey's head of state. A YouTuber in Scotland is convicted of a hate crime for teaching his girlfriend's pug to raise its paw in the Nazi salute. In the United Kingdom police monitor social media for thought crime. And in Canada the case of a comedian who was fined for goofing on a boy with a deformity makes its way all the way up to the Supreme Court! The ruling was 5–4 in the comic's favor. So in Canada they're debating whether you can make fun of a kid with a deformity—in the States we're debating whether you can abort that kid so he can never grow up to be made fun of.

I would often hear, "Trump must be great for comedy, because the jokes write themselves."

In spite of Trump's threats to sue critics, I agree, he was great for comedy. Whether you want to admit it or not, Trump was endlessly entertaining—often times much funnier than the people getting paid to make fun of him. I'm not saying Trump didn't deserve a lot of his lambasting, but what became clear is that The Resistance couldn't get enough of him. They needed Orange Man Bad. So they got lazy and let "the jokes write themselves." And *that*, ladies and gentlemen, was really great for comedy!

Because, while mainstream late-night hosts, stand-ups, sketch comedians, podcasters, and tweeters were all cannibalizing the same orange, small-hands, Russian pee-tape material, it gave comedians like myself the opportunity to take on subjects they wouldn't touch.

On the occasions when I did nibble at the same bloated spray-tanned corpse, I challenged myself to be original—to not allow the jokes to "write themselves."

When Trump was finally out of office you could sense a type of mourning on the part of his most vocal critics in entertainment. Now instead of mourning the exit of their hero, Obama, they were mourning the exit of their supervillain, Trump—with no hope of him ever returning to public office, no matter what that pillow guy said about him being reinstated on August 13th[7].

So, what were they gonna do now? Without Trump, how would their audiences know when to laugh?

* * *

One night, months into the Biden administration, I booked a spot on a friend's show in the City. It was the first time I had performed in Manhattan in a while. I don't remember which COVID-19 variant we were up to. I had been hunkered down in my house—having moved out of Brooklyn to the wilderness of New Jersey—dealing with basement flooding, faults in the foundation, the joy of seeing deer trespass on my property, and the fear that the tics riding on them would make their way under my skin. It felt good to be making the trek in for a stand-up gig and leaving country life behind for a few hours.

---

7   Maybe it'll happen next August 13th?

I was up second in the lineup and caught the first comic's set. She was a young Black woman and working out this bit about going to therapy. One of the things she mentioned was having asked her therapist, a white female, if she had voted for Trump.

Her therapist said she did not vote for Trump—which put the comedian at ease and the audience too. It was the safe move and expected.

But, I thought, comedy is about the unexpected. "Dating is hard" is an unoriginal setup, but you can go anywhere from there. Original or unoriginal. (Also, dating is *not* hard—unless you're pregnant[8]).

On my drive home I was consumed with the other comic's bit. I thought it would be strengthened if she had defied expectation and gone with the idea that she, a young Black female New Yorker, actually *wants* a therapist who voted for Trump.

Why?

Because if your MAGA therapist is honest enough to admit to her Black female patient that she voted for Trump, then you know she's going to be honest with you about all the issues you're working through in therapy.

Starting with that premise, think of all the honest assessments the therapist could give this woman. She could be telling her patient a lot of shit her patient doesn't want to hear or confront. Which opens up even more comedic possibilities.

"We're not at the point where I'm comfortable with this white MAGA bitch calling me the N-word," the comedian may confess. "But we're getting there. That's what healing is all about."

---

8   Ask my pregnant wife.

Now, it is much easier to critique the work of others than it is to hold yourself to the same standard. I know that. So consider this a note to self:

Take a chance. The joke might not land. But no one's gonna arrest you for it. Not here.

* * *

Safety will be the death of comedy. And it seems like the least safe of comedians are all dying.

Comedy legend Norm Macdonald died from cancer on September 14, 2021. Fellow legends Mort Sahl and Paul Mooney passed away that year too. As I write this, Bob Saget, Louie Anderson, and Gilbert Gottfried are no more.[9] Chances are when you found out about these deaths you were in the middle of bingeing clips of Norm on YouTube.

Just a minute ago: Norm was on *The View* calling Bill Clinton a murderer and pissing off Barbara Walters; he was performing an antiroast with lines from an old-timey joke book at The Roast of Bob Saget; and he was butchering O.J. Simpson on "Weekend Update"—and now he's gone? How can that be?

Even before his death Norm had achieved a kind of immortality—captured forever on Conan O'Brien's couch. Eternally funny.

There is the obvious shock of someone passing away who, if you're my age, has existed as long as you have been alive. And sixty-one—the age Norm was when he went—doesn't feel as far away from me as it used to. Or Saget's sixty-five or Gottfried's sixty-seven or Anderson's sixty-eight. Shit—even Mooney's seventy-nine and Sahl's ninety-five feel closer!

---

9   I gotta get this manuscript in before more comedians die!

But what was even more shocking about Norm's death is that he kept the cancer that killed him hidden for nine years—from the public and even his friends. Unlike other comedians who would have milked the sympathy that a cancer diagnosis brings, Norm had the dignity not to give in to that sort of manipulative thing. (Although that one-man show would have been amazing! I would have loved to have seen Norm expand his bit on bowel cancer for *Norm Macdonald Has Cancer: So You Better Laugh!*)

Now, *I* am no Norm MacDonald. Trust me, if I had cancer I would make sure you knew about it—on page one. And I would remind you every few pages too. Don't get me wrong—I'd add some punch lines. At least I'd like to think I would.

Years ago when I found out my mother had cancer I asked the audience at a gig if it meant I'd have to run a marathon now. Like, is that the next stage after denial? At the time I wasn't prepared for either her cancer nor my run.[10]

Comedy can be a powerful way to deal with trauma, darkness, and danger. The more traumatic, darker, and dangerous the subject matter, the more difficult it is to make it funny—but when it works, man, it's like magic.

Although something you may have noticed in recent years is the move away from using comedy to sublimate trauma into something *funny* and just presenting the trauma. Which isn't good for comedy...because it's *not comedy*?

I was on a show a few years back at a boutique comedy club in Astoria, Queens. Alright, it was a coffee shop with a stage in the back. It was a mixed show—with stand-up comics and storytellers. With my ten minutes I was going

---

10 Don't worry. My mother beat cancer—twice. If she hadn't, you would know. And the farthest I've ever run is a half-marathon. It's gonna take some doing in the tragedy department to get me to commit to a full one.

to tell this goofy story about how when I was newly single I thought it would be a good idea to buy a couple of vibrators and stow them at my apartment. You know, to entertain the ladies back at my bachelor pad. If you think dating is hard, *girl*, do I have the solution for you!

What ensues is a tale of sexual misadventure with two double-A battery-powered sex toys ("The Twins," I named them) and some weirded-out dates asking the obvious questions, like "…*What*?"

I was running the set over in my head when the storyteller before me got up on stage and recounted for all in attendance her sexual assault…in painful, violent, heartbreaking detail.

Let's just say she was a hard act to follow:

"So," I began. "…Dating is hard."

This went down years before Hannah Gadsby discussed her own rape in her 2018 Netflix special, *Nanette*.

Like the storyteller in Astoria, Gadsby did not pepper her account of that horrific life event with jokes.

Now I am not accusing Gadsby of being a trauma thief. Unfortunately, far too many women have similar stories of sexual assault to tell. How many of them have the strength or willingness to tell their stories though? Or the audience to subject to them?

I admit that I jumped on the anti-Gadsby bandwagon without having watched her whole special. I had judged her based entirely from a few clips my friends wouldn't stop sending me. But I finally brought myself to watch *Nanette* in its entirety—being the responsible author that I am—and, I offer my sincerest apologies to my red-pilled readers: there are jokes[11] in *Nanette* that I liked.

---

11 NB: they were jokes.

For example, when she's talking about the celebration of Mardi Gras, Gadsby, the ever-awkward lesbian autist asks, "Where do the quiet gays go?"

She even has issues with the Pride flag[12]—with its "very shouty, assertive colors."

Gadsby's follow-up special, *Douglas*, is funnier than *Nanette*—or at least has more jokes than *Nanette* has—and she even takes the opportunity to reveal the trick she played in *Nanette*.

See, she used her stand-up comedy to get her audience to sit around long enough so she could force her stories of rape and other violations onto them.

At the beginning of *Douglas* Gadsby asks, "If you're here because of *Nanette*—why?" to earned laughter.

If you're expecting more trauma in *Douglas*, Gadsby wants you to know that she put all her "trauma eggs into one basket" with the last special.

I wondered why Gadsby chose to do *Nanette* to her comedy audience?

In both of her specials, Gadsby connects her trauma and identity to these grand narratives of comedy, art history[13], and, well, typical woke bullshit. Her talk includes authoritative takes on punching up vs. punching down, truth to power, and identity politics.[14]

There's an academic feel to her stuff. She looks the part of a lecturer—with her eyeglasses and two-piece suit.

---

12 The original Pride flag—the rainbow one. Not the new "more-inclusive" uglier one.

13 She opens *Douglas* with a summary of her setlist, letting the audience know what they're in for and what to be on the lookout for. She ends the special with a slideshow presentation of art masterpieces—and a really weak Louis C.K. joke, followed by an unearned mic drop that she had briefed the audience on at the beginning.

14 I'm writing about all that stuff too. The difference is I'm right.

She looks "smart," you know. But the stuff she's saying isn't smart. It often has the ring of a freshman gender studies essay. There's always the Patriarchy and straight white men, and she absolutely hates Pablo Picasso.

An interesting thing about Gadsby are the targets she chooses for her specials. In *Douglas* she really sticks it to *Where's Waldo?* and the Teenage Mutant Ninja Turtles. In *Nanette* it's cubist painter Picasso and other powerful (not fictional) men. Every one of them safe targets.

In *Nanette* we learn that Picasso was forty-two when he had an affair with a seventeen-year-old girl. As Gadsby puts it, "Picasso fucked an underage girl" and he said, "'It was perfect—I was in my prime and she was in her prime.'"

By today's standards, yeah that's scandalous, but Picasso was with high-school junior Marie-Thérèse back in what, 1927? Nearly one hundred years ago. Gadsby's bit is anachronistic. The historical and cultural context isn't important though. What is important is somehow finding a way to link misogynist Pablo Picasso to a number of other high-profile dudes on the douchebag spectrum—with the worst of them being, of course, The Donald. The safest target ever. Hitler being a distant second.

You know, sometimes trying to go deep just ends up bringing you way out of your depth.

Take Gadsby's defense of Monica Lewinsky in *Nanette*. Gadsby is correct that Lewinsky "used to be an easy punch line." Looking back now, I was a kid in the '90s, it is really messed up how Lewinsky was treated. But here is how Gadsby holds up that mirror to American society[15]—with a particular callout of those who run the comedy game:

---

15   In *Douglas* Gadsby says "Americans are like the straight white men of cultures." Which is funny. But also kind of dumb, since the US is the most diverse country on the planet. How's the saying go, "Give me your tired, your poor, your huddled masses yearning to be straight white men"?

> Maybe, if comedians had done their job properly, and made fun of the man who abused his power, then perhaps we might have had a middle-aged woman with an appropriate amount of experience in the White House, instead, as we do, a man who openly admitted to sexually assaulting vulnerable young women because he could.

Lewinsky was so moved by this that she and the Kiwi comic[16] came together on stage at an event for *Vanity Fair* to discuss "Dealing with Trauma in the Public Eye."

The whole thing is kind of weird, isn't it?

Because, obviously the man Gadsby is referring to—the one "who openly admitted to sexually assaulting vulnerable young women because he could" is President Donald Trump.

But "the man who abused his power" in Gadsby's Lewinsky bit is...President Bill Clinton.

I repeat: Hannah Gadsby is talking about Bill Clinton. The Bill Clinton. You know, The "I did not have sexual relations with that woman" Bill Clinton. The "What does the word 'is' mean?" Bill Clinton. The Bill Clinton who penetrated Lewinsky's twenty-two-year-old vagina with a cigar. Yeah—that guy.

So if my math checks out that would make the "middle-aged woman with an appropriate amount of experience [who should be] in the White House" *Hillary Clinton*—the same Hillary Clinton who was First Lady to...Bill Clinton.

You know, while comics were ripping Lewinsky jokes every day Hillary was calling the former White House intern a "narcissistic loony toon."

---

16   Gadsby is from New Zealand, where, as I learned from Gadsby's routine, New Zealanders and Americans use different words for the same things. Basically New Zealanders use British words but with a dumber accent.

That's the woman Gadsby wanted in the White House?[17]

Because with Hillary in the White House you would still have "the man who abused his power" in the White House—except this time around Bill Clinton would be demoted to the First Man, I guess. That'll show him! Move Bill back in to the home where he has so many fond memories.

Even Lewinsky didn't pick up on the irony of Gadsby's bit. I mean, I highly doubt the middle-aged woman Gadsby was referring to was 2016 Republican presidential candidate Carly Fiorina.

* * *

No one is above criticism. Not even comedians. Your jokes are fair play. And if and when you go deep—whether it be with your personal trauma or political and cultural commentary—you should expect to be criticized.

Dave Chappelle is another comic that often goes deep. He is, of course, much funnier than Gadsby—we're talking by magnitudes of hilarious. After all he is possibly the greatest living comedian. But even *He* is not immune from making goofy commentary.

I think back to *The Bird Revelation* that was filmed at The Comedy Store in Los Angeles. Chappelle closes out that special by talking about a story he read in a book by Iceberg Slim called *Pimp: The Story of My Life*. Chappelle even has the book brought to the stage.[18]

Chappelle has a godly presence when holding a mic. And when he speaks it is with such gravitas—no doubt

---

17   In an alternate reality Gadsby gets her wish: Hillary wins the election. And *Saturday Night Live*'s Kate McKinnon dons the white power suit one more time to sing John Lennon's "Imagine" in honor of madam president's win.

18   For a moment Dave Chappelle is a prop comic.

strengthened by a voice that's gotten gravelly over the years from smoke.

Chappelle gives the *Pimp* CliffsNotes, describing the relationship between Iceberg and one of his "bitches." It's moving, interesting, and a serious presentation of the dark side of humanity.

Finally, Chappelle concludes the traumatic tale with a declaration: "That's the motherfucking capitalist manifesto and that's why I went to South Africa."

That is, why Chappelle walked away all those years ago from a $50 million deal with Comedy Central. See, Chappelle's relationship with the cable network was like the relationship between Iceberg and the victim he was sex trafficking.

It sounds so deep…But it's just not true.

That is, the involuntary relationship between the pimp and his enslaved bitch is not capitalism. Again: it's involuntary. Unlike the relationship between Chappelle and Comedy Central—which was capitalism. As is the relationship between Chappelle and Netflix. So much so that in response to Chappelle's last (and perhaps final) controversial special, *The Closer*, a headline in *The Advocate* reads: "Netflix's Dave Chappelle Debacle Shows It Puts Capitalism Over People."

In *The Closer*, Chappelle addresses his critics who have been accusing him of transphobia, among other transgressions, over the years.

I don't know how many of these critics even bothered to watch *The Closer*—or if they did, how they failed to see what I saw. Because at the end of the special Chappelle manages to tell an incredible story about his dear friend, a transgender woman named Daphne Dorman, who (spoiler) committed suicide.

I won't give too much away other than to say that Chappelle, a master of his craft, was able to express this particular story of trauma with both humanity and a lot of funny fucking jokes.[19]

---

19 When it works, man, it's like magic.

But the demands for (social) justice haven't stopped. Even Hannah Gadsby complained that "Dave gets $20 million to process his emotionally stunted partial world view"—much more dough than she gets to process hers.[20] And in response, Chappelle demanded in part that her fans admit that she's not funny.

What a wacky timeline we're living on, huh—where Dave Chappelle and Hannah Gadsby are beefing!

The tension between these two comics is a pretty good metaphor for the state of comedy today. Believe me: Comedy is most certainly not dead. People continue to turn to comedians—whether it's to laugh, or to be preached to, or to share in someone else's trauma (jokes or no jokes).

Sure, there is a lot of shit being made—and please stop sending it to me!—but there is also a lot of great stuff going on too. Some of it is in this book.

But no matter what happens in comedy or in the world or how many pages of mine you manage to get through, we can all be thankful that there will always be clips of Norm Macdonald for us to rewatch. Never stop sending me links to those. It's one way to keep comedy alive. Keep reading for more ways.

20　*That's* the motherfucking capitalist manifesto!

HOW I BECAME A
"FAR-RIGHT RADICAL"

At the end of 2020, I was put on a list—and not a good one. It wasn't the *Hollywood Reporter*'s Next Gen Class or *Forbes*'s 30 Under 30 or Top 10 Comedians Who Should Be Famous By Now.

Forget the accolades—I would take just being under thirty again. That would have been so much better for my career than where I was: a comedian approaching forty, who found his work labeled "far-right" in an academic paper titled "Evaluating the scale, growth, and origins of right-wing echo chambers on YouTube."

Although I wasn't mentioned by name, if you turned to the last page of the preprint paper—which meant it had yet to be peer-reviewed or submitted to a journal, but was still out there for public consumption—you would see the words "We the Internet TV" huddled among other supposedly far-right YouTube channels.

I was the head writer and producer of We the Internet TV before my position was eliminated on October 14, 2020. For five years, up until my shit-canning, I was responsible for making hundreds of comedy videos about current events, politics, and culture. My mug and essence is all over WTI.

Some of my hits include comedy sketches like "Stop Making Me Defend Donald Trump," "ESL Students Learn New Gender Pronouns," and "Social Justice Warrior Therapist."

I remember the good old days of cancel culture, when if you landed a gig on a major show like *Saturday Night Live* or *Jeopardy!* someone would have to put in some work to get you canceled. Before online mobs could be whipped up in seconds and get you trending, a bitter pest would have to comb through your tweets, listen to hours of your podcast, or track down a recording of you bombing at an open mic to find the material to take you down.

Don't get me wrong: My "problematic" material is out there. And it's right here—in these pages. You'll often hear public figures complain that they've been taken out of context—and rightfully so. But I might be the only person who sounds worse *in context*.

My friend Noam Dworman, who owns the Comedy Cellar, shared the study with me. We had a laugh about the ridiculousness of it. As a frequent guest on his and our friend Hatem Gabr's podcast *Live from America*, I asked him how it felt to be "far-right adjacent"?

Noam encouraged me to respond to the charge.[21] And the more I thought about it, the more pissed off I got. This study eliminated the need for a critic of mine to put in the legwork of even a keyword search. No, researchers from prestigious institutions like the University of Pennsylvania and

---

21 Noam introduced me to James Taranto at *The Wall Street Journal*, where an earlier version of this story was first printed.

Harvard had already gone to the trouble of demonstrating that I was somehow responsible for "the phenomenon of right-wing radicalization on YouTube."

Who the fuck wants to work with *that guy*?

Which videos made me a far-right radical? I wondered. I wanted to scroll through the WTI library with my accusers and point out the kind of "far-right" material that won us a Webby Award in 2017 for Best Film & Video in the Variety category. Other winners that year included the Women's March organization, which took home the Social Movement Webby. CNN's Van Jones picked up a Special Achievement Webby for promoting diversity. There was also some chick whose gown had "I ♥ Abortion" written all over it (literally, from neck to toe). I don't remember what award she won, but it probably had something to do with loving abortion. The Webby Awards are not exactly a celebration of "far-right" radicalism.[22]

At first, I found it odd that the words "fascism," "racism," and "terrorism" were missing from the paper, because these terms have become inextricably linked to the far right. Then I realized it was a smart (and cowardly) move on the part of the authors to leave them out: just use the umbrella term "far-right" and allow your readers to fill in the tacit -*isms*. That way, you don't risk being called out for labeling people who are not fascists, racists, and terrorists fascists, racists, and terrorists.

Instead, the study was peppered with nebulous adjectives like "extreme" and "radical"—which allow readers to see their own bogeymen.

I'm not the only one who took issue with being mislabeled. In the study's view, former Evergreen College professor

---

22 Aside from anti-Semitism, the far-right and leaders of the Women's March don't have that much in common.

Bret Weinstein—a self-described progressive and Bernie Sanders supporter—was far-right too. To be fair: I did share the stage with Bret when I took my minidocumentary *Five Reasons Why We Need Hate Speech* on the road to Portland. Perhaps some of my far-right funk rubbed off on him and the two women who joined us on the panel: Bret's wife and partner, Heather Heying, and journalist Katie Herzog.

The study also gave far-right stamps of disapproval to neuroscientist Sam Harris (a self-confessed liberal and staunch anti-Trumper), podcast host, comedian, and UFC color commentator Joe Rogan (who considers himself "pretty liberal"—no matter how much tar his critics try to throw on him), and even Bloggingheads.tv (whose regular contributors included *Vox* co-founder Ezra Klein).

Even Mark Ledwich, whom the paper's authors thanked for sharing data with them, took issue with "the way the labels were converted into far-right and far-left." (Funny enough: on his site Transparency.Tube, which tracks political channels on YouTube, We the Internet TV only scored "Right" and "Anti-woke" at the time.)

Lumping together all these creators with vastly different political persuasions was lazy at best. At worst it undermined criticism of actual far-right content—if you can even find it on the platform. As YouTuber Rebel Wisdom put it, "if everything is far right, then nothing is." He was, of course, also "far right" by the paper's standards.

It's the type of analysis you'd have to be living in an echo chamber to come up with—you know, academia. The authors wrote that "the growing appeal of radical content on YouTube may simply reflect a more general trend driven by a complicated combination of causes, both technological and sociological, that extend beyond the scope of the platform's algorithms."

Now I can't speak for all those other "radical" YouTube channels. But when it came to my work at We the Internet TV, its "growing appeal" had a lot to do with it being funny. I even dared to do the type of comedy that gets you put on lists.

* * *

When my response to the paper was published in *The Wall Street Journal* I got some pushback on Twitter that went something like this:

"*Whaaa*! 'Cancel culture!' Quit whining, snowflake!"

Of course, there's a difference between "whining" and "setting the record straight." (And people are still using "snowflake"? Really?) If someone doesn't want to work with me, I want it to be because of something I actually said, or did, or wrote in *this* book you're reading. I might be an asshole, guys, but I'm not a "far-right" asshole. No marches with tiki torches for me.

Surely these commenters could understand what it's like to be mislabeled. I figure that's why so many of them put their pronouns in their bio.

When I sat down to write this book I made sure to reach out to the paper's authors. In an email one of them apologized to me for the initial error and offered an explanation. They had "made the far-right category too large" in the preprint edition and fixed it after "a number of people pointed out this error."

It looks like all that whining paid off!

My old YouTube channel, the author writes, "along with the other channels you mention, are now classified as 'anti-woke,' which more accurately captures how they were labeled by prior authors and I hope strikes you as more accurate also."

It does. (Read on. You'll see why.)

The published version of the study appears online in *PNAS* (*Proceedings of the National Academy of Sciences of the United States of America*)—which sounds super serious.

The title of the paper has been changed to a less-provocative one: "Examining the consumption of radical content on YouTube."[23] And the table that lists channels by name is no longer included.

As the author told me, "I would say that this is an example of science working the way it's supposed to."

Sure. But the science is behind a paywall. I had to shell out ten dollars to read it, while the preprint is still free to read and available to the public.[24] Few people give a shit about corrections anyway—let alone enough to part with a Hamilton for the pleasure of reading them. And this study is anything but a pleasure to read. It's dense and way out of my field of expertise.[25] Had my work not been listed in the original, I wouldn't have spent the time or money on the published version. I could really use that ten bucks right now!

That's not to say there isn't some good news in the published paper. Here's a glimpse behind the paywall:

> We also find that the antiwoke community, while still small compared with left and centrist communities, is larger than the far right and is growing over time, both in size and engagement. We find evidence that the anti-woke community draws members from the far-right more than from any other polit-

---

23 Here's the link: https://www.pnas.org/content/118/32/e2101967118
24 Here's the cheap link: https://arxiv.org/pdf/2011.12843.pdf
25 Fortunately, I had members of my community on Locals to help dumb it down for me.

ical community, and that antiwoke members show an affinity for far-right content off-platform. On the other hand, when they leave, antiwoke members are more likely to move to left, center, and right than far right. Thus, while there do seem to be links between the antiwoke and far-right communities in terms of the content they consume, the hypothesized role of antiwoke channels as a gateway to far right is not supported. Rather, it seems more accurate to describe antiwoke as an increasingly popular—and sticky—category of its own. The implications of this fact are beyond the scope of this paper and left for future work to explore.

I'll lay down one implication, as I see it: You don't have to be far-right to be antiwoke. And that is good news!

The more people realize this, the more willing others will be to openly reject the wokeness and the more fun we will all have mocking it without fear of being mislabeled.

PANDEMIC DADDY

I love my wife and son.

But I have thought of abandoning them.

Because single mothers are heroes.

And what kind of man would I be to stand in the way of my wife becoming a hero?

The best way for me to fight the Patriarchy is to stop being a patriarch.

* * *

What I miss most about Brooklyn Heights is walking. My wife and I took frequent strolls through the neighborhood. One Sunday I think we left the apartment five times to take a different route. When she was pregnant with our first, the further along into her pregnancy she got, the more her pace slowed and the distance we traveled shortened. But any amount of time outside was important.

When the weather is right in New York City, you forget about how most of the year it's awful. With the right amount of sun, air, and humor you can even forget that you're living through a pandemic.

"I can't believe you're bringing a child into the world during a plague!" one might say.

Well, can you think of a better time to repopulate the Earth?

We brought our son home from the hospital—normally they hold mommy and baby for forty-eight hours, but with COVID-19 creeping around they were released twenty-four hours earlier than usual.

In the days following his birth we made sure to continue our walks. We had a third wheel now to slow us down, but he was in a Doona: an infant car seat that also transforms into a stroller. So with alternate-side parking rules suspended indefinitely and no telling what future mayoral decrees may bring, we were ready to collapse the stroller, strap it into the backseat of our Honda, and hightail it out of the city if we felt the heat around the corner.

One morning on our way to the Promenade my wife and I noticed that the gate to the Pierrepont Playground was chained shut. Sure, our son was too small to play on any of the equipment. But even though we sometimes felt like we were the last people on Earth, we knew that wasn't the case. There were other children out there—stuck indoors—because good people "followed the science" and closed down the monkey bars.

The playgrounds were finally reopened in late June, with dog parks to follow. I sat on a bench outside the Pierrepont playground one afternoon with my son in my arms. The playground was filled with kids of all ages and adults wearing face-coverings.

Inequality is real! I thought, looking at the adults. *Some parents aren't wealthy enough to afford au pairs from Europe, so they have to settle for nannies from Central America.*

An old woman sitting on a bench next to ours got my attention. She was in love with my son, she said, and wanted to take him home.

It would be easy to go down the creepy path—go down that way if you want to—but that's not what this was about.

This woman was in her eighties and had been locked up inside her home for the past few months. It would drive me crazy, I know, but she was all there. COVID-19 really had it out for people her age—and I'm sure she knew that—but the playgrounds were open again. It was perfect outside. And she had just met a gorgeous lil' baby named Andreas.

I noticed she wore her blue surgical mask around her neck and had a hardcover book with her. I was maskless too and asked her what she was reading.

It was *Fear: Trump in the White House* by Bob Woodward.

Oh no! I thought. *Please don't let this be the last book this woman reads before she dies!*[26]

No, I hadn't read the book—and I still haven't—but I had spent years watching people allow Donald Trump to consume their lives. Funny people stopped being funny and started being "brave." Entire personas online centered on being blocked by the 45th president of the United States. And somehow Trump was responsible for, among many things, the nation's mental health crisis, lack of sex, and at least one hurricane.

At Aretha Franklin's funeral service in 2018, Michael Eric Dyson took the opportunity to destroy Trump.

---

26   Let *That Joke Isn't Funny Anymore* be the last book she reads before she dies.

"You lugubrious leech," he said. "You dopey doppelgänger of deceit and deviance, you lethal liar, you dim-witted dictator, you foolish fascist."

I found it unfortunate that Dyson chose to hammer Trump at the funeral for the Queen of Soul. What was also unfortunate was that he used the word "doppelgänger" incorrectly.

Doppelgänger is an apparition or double of a living person. It's not an apparition or double of an idea.

So, something like "deceit and deviance incarnate" would have been correct. Or if you're going for rhythm *and* meaning, something like, "You insipid incarnation of deceit and deviance...." I think that would have gone well with Dyson's "orange apparition."

While Dyson was applauded for destroying Trump, the president was the real winner. The man managed to crash the celebration of one diva's incredible life without even being there.

If Trump was the "orange apparition" of which Dyson spoke, you can blame Dyson's own words for summoning it.

When it comes time for my funeral, it better be all about me.

I spoke with the old woman on the bench for some time. I could tell it had been awhile since her last conversation with someone. It was like that with a lot of people coming out of lockdown. Before I left, I wanted to give her a hug— but I knew letting her hold my son would mean more to her.

I couldn't do that though. Not because of social distancing. But because my wife and I had a whole roster of quarantined loved ones who had yet to hold our baby. It wouldn't be right.

So, I asked the old woman if she would like to touch my son's feet.

Without waiting for her to answer, I took off his socks and put them in my pocket.

I held him in front of her and she took his feet, one in each hand. She was gentle. She wanted to take him home.

It's amazing how much joy one baby's existence can bring into the world.

I thanked her and brought my son back home to our one-bedroom apartment.

From time to time I think about that old woman. My son has grown a lot since then—he's been walking longer than he crawled—but his feet still have that ridiculous baby magic to them. I'm fortunate to have them nearby.

During the plague I became a pandemic daddy, lost my job, buried a friend, was labelled a "far-right radical," then unlabeled, went a little crazy, sold an apartment in BK, and bought a house in the sticks.

As I type this, my family is not living in that house in the sticks, because it is currently gutted and unlivable. So we're crammed in with my in-laws, while I work on this book and hope to finish it before our new baby arrives.

Yeah, my wife is pregnant again—we are taking this repopulate-the-planet thing seriously. And in the coming months I'm gonna need more happy baby feet. I'm a comedian after all and trying to figure out my future prospects.

While the pandemic and the responses to it hurt far too many people, I am one of the fortunate ones. I grew—as a husband, a father, and a comedian. Some days I feel like an outlier. Because those who went insane under Trump have stayed insane. If Trump broke you, Biden can't fix you.

Even though we moved out of Brooklyn Heights I've kept my account on the Nextdoor app, so I can check in on my old neighborhood. I read that there's a "Parking Menace" on one block, hogging multiple spots, and a "Phantom Shitter" on the other, who marks their territory on the sidewalk. A Spotted Lanternfly was spotted in the 'hood and an unleashed pit bull too. Concerned residents are asking questions, like how to deal with homeless men chasing after you; when, if ever, to call the police on a person of color; and "Public Shaming Etiquette" when it comes to masks.

I am happy to be out. If you think it takes a village to raise a child, you better be real picky about who you let into your village.

What's clear is that the same people who ruined Facebook are ruining Nextdoor—shitty people who take pride in not living their lives and do all they can to inject themselves and their strain of politics into yours and mine.

A flier taped to a lamppost near the Brooklyn-Queens Expressway was promoting a community get-together—catered by Bakers Against Racism. According to Dr. Ibram X. Kendi, author of *How to Be an Antiracist*, you're either an antiracist baker or you're a racist baker. There is no such thing as a "not-racist" baker. Keep that in mind the next time you're buying a black-and-white cookie from that spot in Carroll Gardens.

I got an email from a local restaurant my wife and I used to frequent. It reads in part (emphases mine):

> Now as we more actively pursue the imperfect work of *unpacking our own privilege* we are revising our sense of purpose *in the face of systemic racism* and *white supremacy*. This is work we have supported over the years, but

we haven't been sufficiently resolute in *prioritizing antiracism* as a practice. We are grateful for the Black activists and our *colleagues of color* whose efforts have built the framework for becoming *more effective allies*.

Bro... I thought. *You're a restaurant.*

I know it's hard enough to run a business under normal conditions. Imagine trying to do it during a pandemic with government-mandated lockdowns and Kafkaesque regulations. So many restaurants were hurting. Some managed to eke out a few more months of hurt before closing for good.

But "prioritizing antiracism as a practice"—along with the other woke boilerplate I highlighted above—aren't the ingredients to help a restaurant achieve what should be its primary goal: to make food people will pay to eat.

The last time my wife and I ate at this place, I don't remember if the dishes were sufficiently antiracist, but I do remember them being more than sufficiently salty. You're not going to make a dent in systemic racism and white supremacy with all that sodium. (Although you might raise the blood pressure on what's left of your primarily white bougie clientele.)

Whatever your activism is, nobody wants to be force-fed it. Especially if it's a humorless, joyless, anti-life dish that sucks the taste out of everything.

4

DR. IBRAM X. KENDI
IS CANCEL PROOF[27]

n January 25, 2021 Dr. Ibram X. Kendi, author of *How to Be an Antiracist* and the children's book *Antiracist Baby*, took part in a conversation with the New York State Association of Independent Schools on the topic of "How to Be an Antiracist School." I am only aware that this eseminar took place because an "EXCLUSIVE CLIP" allegedly from it was shared on Twitter.

In the clip Kendi speaks for less than a minute and recounts for those in attendance via Zoom how, in his words:

> I think it was last week my daughter came
> home and said she wanted to be a boy. You
> know, which was horrifying for my wife to
> hear—myself to hear. And so, of course, we're

27   A version of this chapter was first published in *Spiked* as "Why Ibram X Kendi won't be cancelled."

like, "Okay, what affirmative messages about
girlhood, you know, can we be teaching her
to protect her from whatever she's hearing in
our home or even outside of our home that
would make her want to be a boy?"

Kendi goes on to draw a parallel to the messages that
children—both of-color and white—may be hearing about
race and the impact that messaging might be having on the
young ones' perceived identities. But the portion I quote
above got the most attention. As expected.

Here you have the antiracist guru himself, Dr. Kendi,
saying something that could be interpreted as transphobic!
He chose to use the word "horrifying," after all. As model
and activist Munroe Bergdorf puts it on her Instagram
"Transphobia = White Supremacy." And white supremacy is
antithetical to antiracism. And antiracism is a cornerstone of
wokeism. Which creates a huge problem:

Can there be antiracist transphobes?

How are Kendi's woke allies to respond? Will there be
book burnings? Parents in Park Slope using Kendi's *Antiracist Baby* for kindling?

Now, as you know, I am by no means a woke ally, and
as much as I enjoy watching their infighting I still don't like
the ease with which livelihoods are destroyed online. There's
a reason why Kendi's trans comments were getting attention—even for the brief half-life of a tweet—and it's because
the person who chose to upload the less-than-a-minute-long
segment chose to bring it to the public's attention.

I never managed to track down a complete recording of
the eseminar. When I contacted NYSAIS, I was informed
that one was not available at the time. So unless you were
one of the lucky few who attended the event live—or have

a Zoom link to the replay—all you have to go on are those fifty seconds or so of Kendi speaking. Context, clarifications, and intentions unknown. (I slid into @RadCentrism's DMs—the Twitter account that shared the clip—to ask for the full footage, but Rad never got back to me.)

But the intentions of the video's uploader are clear. In a number of follow-up tweets in the thread, @RadCentrism tagged transgender activists and organizations, and even *TMZ* and *The View*. It was no doubt a provocation and challenge to Kendi's allies to "come get your boy" and do to him what they would do to any of their ideological enemies: rip him the fuck apart!

But as far as I can tell, no one on Kendi's side ever took the bait. I saw no civil war brewing. And still no cancellation on the horizon.

To be clear: I don't want to see the man cancelled over his supposed trans transgression. Instead, I'd like to see his ideas exposed for the garbage that they are and let those in the supposed marketplace of ideas respond accordingly. I think mockery is the appropriate response to Kendi and this motherfucker has given us so much to mock!

Do you remember Kendi inveighing against Supreme Court Justice Amy Coney Barrett—who at the time was still a nominee—for her crime of adopting Black children while being white? Behold one of Kendi's amicus tweets:

> Some White colonizers "adopted" Black children. They "civilized" these "savage" children in the "superior" ways of White people, while using them as props in their lifelong pictures of denial, while cutting the biological parents of these children out of the picture of humanity.

His criticism of Barrett's family is gross, but what's even worse is his proposal for an amendment to the US Constitution that "would make unconstitutional racial inequity over a certain threshold, as well as racist ideas by public officials (with "racist ideas" and "public official" clearly defined)."

"Clearly defined" coming from Kendi is hilarious! Consider his "clearly defined" definition of racism—one of "our fundamental definitions," as he puts it in *How to Be an Antiracist*:

> Racism is a powerful collection of racist policies that lead to racial inequity and are substantiated by racist ideas.

I am not making this up.

His definition of "race" is even better—and from the same book:

> RACE: A power construct of collected or merged difference that lives socially.

I am not *constructing* this!

The dude has got to be trolling! I appreciate a good troll, but I want the good (not a real) doctor to keep *me* and *my* out of "we" and "our." This is Kendi's ideology—and these are his dumb definitions—which calls to "establish and permanently fund the Department of Anti-racism (DOA)."

The DOA would be "empowered with disciplinary tools to wield over and against policymakers and public officials who do not voluntarily change their racist policy and ideas." Thankfully Kendi's clearly unconstitutional DOA is DOA—as I'm sure Justice Barrett and the other Justices without adopted Black children would unanimously agree.

But totalitarians can still dream, can't they?

I am amazed that Kendi has managed to get this far in life. We're talking about a public intellectual whose whole schtick is to reduce the complexity of human action and interaction—and the results thereof—to a dualism: they (and therefore you) are either racist or antiracist. There is no such thing, according to Kendi, as "not racist." It's not permanent though. It changes moment to moment. You're racist over here and then—BOOM—you're antiracist over there. That goes for people, policies, and pop-up restaurants.

By Kendi's own rubric, even his daughter's desire to be a boy would need to be unpacked: Is it (or she) racist or antiracist?

Kendi's and his wife's concerns for their daughter: racist or antiracist?

Is even conceiving a child racist or antiracist? (I wanna know before my wife pushes out our next one!)

Yet this level of thought hasn't gotten Kendi laughed out of the room. It's gotten him Boston University's Center for Antiracist Research, not one but multiple *New York Times* Best Sellers, and a MacArthur "Genius" Grant.

Have you read *How to Be an Antiracist*? Because I did. I slogged through every single page of it. It is so poorly written and even more poorly argued—I felt like I was being punished for having learned to read.

Plus, I mistakenly ordered a large-print edition—which means it was even harder for me to skip over words and sentences. And the guy uses "Latinx" a lot! Over and over again—so many Latin-*equis*! It felt like he was trying to start some shit with me on the playground.

Kendi does this odd thing throughout the book, where he describes a system of inequity in the United States, demonstrates how to break free of that system's constraints—the man is living proof of how to do so—yet insists on pushing his bullshit antiracism, instead of promoting the very behaviors that get shit done.

For example, Kendi's parents are married and young Ibram grew up with a father figure in the home. You know, what we call "privileges" now. Those two privileges put Kendi at least four steps ahead in this race called life.

His mother "settled for a corporate career in healthcare technology." His father "settled for an accounting career." As Kendi puts it, "They entered the American middle class—a space then as now defined by its disproportionate White majority."

Woah—in a country that's disproportionately white who would have thought those in the middle-class would be white too?

Kendi wonders though "what would have been if [his] parents had not let their reasonable fears stop them from pursuing their dreams. Traveling Ma helping to free the Black world. Dad accompanying her and finding inspiration for his freedom poetry"—instead of "settling for" corporate careers.

My guess is pursuing careers in "freeing the Black world" and "freedom poetry" would have made it difficult for Kendi's parents to send him to private school.

Look, in college I wanted to be a poet but decided to get serious and pursue a career in comedy instead. Call it "freedom comedy," if you like, but I gotta tell you there are days I wish I had "settled for" work in healthcare or gone the accounting route. Career wise, those are much smarter moves—especially if you want to raise a family. Look at me—I'm on fucking TikTok for Christ's sake!

Both of Kendi's parents, "emerged from poor families" and "fed [him] the mantra that education and hard work would uplift [him], just as it had uplifted them, and would, in the end, uplift all Black people."

Sounds like good advice and common sense. But Kendi calls such values assimilationist or products of white supremacy. One of the worst things antiracism does is deem positive values—that work universally!—the stuff "of Whiteness." Or as Kendi puts it mockingly, "the 'superior' ways of White people."

Call me an assimilationist if you want to, Kendi—but I think "getting off crack, street corners, and government 'handouts'" are good ideas. And I bet those things are at least "partially holding incomes down." Then again, I have no clue how much crack costs today.

I haven't read *Antiracist Baby*, but the adult version reads enough like a children's book. All inequity is due to racism? Seriously? Not individual choices, talents, or even luck? Not even just a little?

Theologians are mocked for using the "God of the gaps" fallacy, wherein anything science has yet to explain must be the work of the divine. Well, the priests of Wokeness have replaced God of the gaps with "Racism of the gaps"—even for phenomena that can be explained rationally.

On page four of his large-print edition for the blind, Kendi writes that in high school he "carried a GPA lower than 3.0" and his "SAT score barely cracked 1000." A few pages later he says, "Of course, intelligence is as subjective as beauty. But I kept using 'objective' standards, like test scores and report cards, to judge myself." The hubris of this guy! (*Hubris* is one of those SAT words.)

Look, I'm a Queens kid too, I almost got a 1400 on my SAT, and I was ranked third in my high school graduating class. Lots of extracurricular activities too. Just a few more correct answers on the SAT was all I needed to get that 1-4-double O!

Sometimes I look back and think, maybe I would have gotten it if Mom hadn't smoked Marlboro Lights and drank Budweisers when she was pregnant with me. (Would a different brand of booze and smokes have enhanced my brain development?)

Other times I think, maybe I would have gotten a 1400 if I didn't have a girlfriend when I took the test. Less time making out and more time doing test prep!

But even with all those *what-ifs?* I know there is a limit to how well I could have done on the test. The issue isn't the test. It's me. And I accept that. I'm smart—but I'm not *Asian* smart! (They rock that standardized shit!)

As a Latino, I guess, I could always blame the System for my failings. Like New York Congressman Jamaal Bowman tweets it, "Standardized testing is a pillar of systemic racism."

Systemic racism has become the new "If you don't know the answer to the question always pick choice C." Which is terrible advice for test-taking and life. (I would love to see Bowman's test scores! Wouldn't you?)

Kendi writes in *How to Be an Antiracist*, "I thought I was stupid, too dumb for college."

No, Kendi, you are definitive proof that no one is too dumb for college.

To be fair: This article he wrote in 2003, when he was in college, under his birth name Ibram *Rogers*, titled "Living with the White Race," is way more enjoyable than Ibram Kendi's antiracist masterpiece.

Peep this (emphasis mine):

> Caucasians make up only 10 percent of the world's population and that small percentage of people have recessive genes. Therefore they're facing extinction. *Whites have tried*

*to level the playing field with the AIDS virus
and cloning,* but they know these deterrents
will only get them so far. This is where the
murder, psychological brainwashing and
deception comes [sic] into play.

Europeans are trying to survive and I can't
hate them for that. However, I'm not going
to just sit back and let them physically,
mentally, socially, spiritually and econom-
ically destroy my people. Although I don't
hate whites, I would still prefer to be in the
field as opposed to the house.

According to *The Famuan* website—published by Florida
A&M University—Ibram's column appeared every Wednesday.
At the time he could "be reached at ibramrogers@aol.com."

An AOL e-mail address! God, I feel old!

But seriously, people, do you really think you are going
to cancel this man? Ibram X. Kendi is cancel-proof!

But that's not to say @RadCentrism's move on Twitter
was all for nothing. There is a great lesson here. Something,
I think, we can all get behind.

As Kendi sums up his ideology in a YouTube video for
Waterstones Booksellers: "When someone supports policies
that create and reproduce racial inequity they're being racist.
When someone supports policies that yield and create racial
equity they're being an antiracist."

As critics like Thomas Chatterton Williams and John
McWhorter have pointed out, had Kendi not been Kendi
he would surely be cancelled for that clip of him on Twitter.
Not to mention his college musings about whites cooking up
HIV and cloning around with nature.

The fact that we have yet to see such a thing take place—and we won't!—can either mean that our society has matured and we are ready to give everyone the benefit of the doubt and are no longer giving in to the basest instincts of cancel culture....

Or more likely: Kendi is right. We are living in a society with "policies that create and reproduce racial inequity" and it sure is working out well for him.

LUIS AMATE PEREZ

Lou Perez is Luis Amate Perez. That's my full name. My publisher insists that I tell you this.

In a world where people pad their résumés with racial, ethnic, and gender identities, we're checking that diversity box as hard as we can. We might even throw up an accent mark over the first "e" in *Pérez* to stress the "*e*" and the point: If you do not buy my book, then you are complicit in systemic racism and whatever else.

I'm waiting to get my DNA results back from 23andMe to see how many people I can guilt on the cellular level into buying my book.

As far as I know, there are only two other men in the United States who share my name. One of them is the man who named me: my father.

Whatever you do, don't confuse us for, nor conflate us with, the countless others named "Luis Perez." I have an excellent credit score, but because I have the same name as these losers, leasing my Honda took way too long. (Background-check yourselves, *Luises*, and get your shit together!)

There was a time though when I felt solidarity with all the Luis Perezes of the world—in particular the L.P.'s of the USA. In fact, I viewed all Latinos and Hispanics as a monolith. You know, in a way weren't we all named "Luis Perez"? It's the same way many mainstream pundits, politicians, and allies still view those of us with Spanish last names.

To be fair: I was young—with no life experience, let alone achievements to call my own. And I was rapt about my father's immigrant story—the odyssey that brought the butcher all the way from San Miguel de Tucumán, Argentina to Queens, New York—without even graduating high school.

Sharing a name with my hero, I put pressure on myself to grow into it. Like, my father didn't make me quote *El Gaucho Martín Fierro*, the Argentine epic poem by José Hernández, for my high school yearbook.

While my peers in the class of 2000 were quoting the musical *Rent* and Blink-182 lyrics, I was spitting these rhymes from the pampas of the 1870s:

> Yo soy toro en mi rodeo
>
> Y torazo en rodeo ajeno;
>
> Siempre me tuve por güeno
>
> Y si me quieren probar
>
> Salgan otros a cantar
>
> Y veremos quién es menos.[28]

---

28 "I am the best of my own at home, And better than best afar; I have won in song my right of place, If any gainsay me;—face to face, Let him come and better me, song for song, Guitar against guitar." — El Gaucho - The Guacho (Edición Bilingüe) from the Edición autorizada por el Instituto Cultural Walter Owen

My high school administration had my Spanish teacher, Brother Victor, read over the lines to make sure they were appropriate to print. Not exactly the poetry of Hoppus, DeLonge, and Raynor: "I guess this is growing up!"

Whether your father is legal or illegal or a citizen, it is great to grow up with him as your hero. Hell, your dad doesn't even have to be your hero. Statistically speaking, just having your dad around is a privilege.

Monica Padman, co-host of the *Armchair Expert* podcast, posted this to her Instagram: "If someone doesn't understand privilege, then show them this video." "This video is old," her caption reads, "but it's endlessly relevant."

In it a cast of teenagers—Black, white, boys, and girls—is lined up on a field. They're going to race for one hundred dollars. But before the race begins the man organizing it—picture a high school football coach in pep-talk mode—is "gonna make a couple statements. If those statements apply to you I want you to take two steps forward. If those statements don't apply to you I want you to stay right where you're at."

The first two statements, each worth two steps forward, are "If both of your parents are still married" and "If you grew up with a father figure in the home."

Some of the other statements that follow are weird. Like, "If you've never had to worry about your cell phone being shut off"—that's worth two steps too. The same as your parents being married. That's sad. In another era it would have been your landline. How many steps is a landline telephone worth?

And the other weird one is "If it wasn't about your athletic ability you don't have to pay for college." My guess is the question was not meant to include academic scholarships. It's more about driving home the point of having parents who can afford to send you to college. Take two steps.

After all the preliminary privilege steps are taken, the race begins and—spoiler—none of the Black kids win it.

So what's the lesson?

According to Coach, "If this were a fair race and everybody was back on that line, I guarantee you some of these Black dudes would smoke you." And "It's only because you have this big of a head start that you are possibly going to win this thing called life."

Now I think that's a terrible message to send to young people—in particular, the Black kids they cast in the video: "You don't have a head start—so you're fucked."

And what was that casting call like?

"We think you're very talented, but the problem is you know who your dad is....So, we're gonna have to pass."

That bit of cynicism and stereotyping aside, I think one message is pretty clear: having married parents and a father figure are good. Unfortunately, they're not the norm—they're privileges now.

You'd expect to see people sharing this video as a way to promote these privileges. "Do these things! Give your kids a head start in life!"

But chances are, if you've ever shared this video you're no privilege skeptic. In fact you probably talk about dismantling the patriarchy and "disrupting the Western-prescribed nuclear family structure," as Black Lives Matter put it at one time on their website.

In short: the video is not the own you think it is. If anything, it's a self-own. And a call for self-ownership.

Growing up, my pops would tell my younger brothers and me that because of our last name we would have to work twice as hard to make it in America.

I did not find that to be the case. But if we were Asian coming up now? Hell yeah!

My dad and my mother no doubt gave us a head start. And even though it might not be true that people are holding you back, it can sometimes motivate you to work as if they are. In the face of great adversity—real and fictional—hone your craft, find your voice, and share it with the world. Become the hero of your own story.

After forty years of hearing my patriarch's stories, I can tell them better than he can. But ultimately they're his stories. Not mine.

If I can't take credit for my own father's accomplishments, how the hell can I take credit for those of Latinos and Hispanics—*mi gente*—collectively? Or for my mother, Florence's, for that matter—and her Irish, Italian, German—Ridgewood, Queens!—ancestors?

Identity is a currency nowadays. If you abide by that trade, you've either hit the lottery or you're in debt. But when I think about who I am, what I find is my most-defining feature, what makes me *me*, and what I identify most strongly as is comedian.

Comedy is the way I've been able to unyoke myself from my otherwise immutable characteristics—you know, my intersecting axes of privilege, domination, and oppression—and woke nonsense. (Some kid is going into debt right now to study that nonsense.)

Comedy influences how I see the world, how I respond to it, and how I choose to present the world back to itself.

My father never told me to play up my last name, but he has told me to be careful of the views I express. He doesn't want to see me blacklisted. He worries. He's cute. He's my dad.

Fortunately, my experience has been the opposite of my father's fears. What I've discovered is that the more outspoken I've become, the more willing I am to express my point of view, to be honest about the person I've become, the more success I've had.

But sometimes I do think, maybe I should hold back—just a little. At least until those 23andMe results come through.

AGED OUT

My heart goes out to all the actors who sucked all the wrong dicks in Hollywood. Those who've slept their way to stardom don't get the credit they deserve. I mean, to do it you still have to be good at sex. I'm sure many of those who didn't make it were good too—they just had bad luck or shitty representation.

It's too late for me to suck my way to the top. Sure, I know some fellas who disagree and would happily guide my head—but they can't guide my career. And the ones who can aren't interested in some forty-year-old's amateur mouth.

Now when I was a young man—when I worked out like a Long Island meathead and had the accent to back up the muscles—that was the time to start sucking my way to a career in showbiz.

I'm telling you: When Luis was an undergrad at New York University, he was a legit piece of ass. I have the pictures to prove it. At age eighteen, a new friend at school asked

Luis if he would like to model for some photographs. There was baby oil—but no money. I did get free prints though.

That shoot marks the only time in my life that I have ever shaved my chest. If you look closely in the photos you can spot two light wreaths of black hair around my nipples—because young Luis had gotten a little shy with the razor.

Later, one of Luis's shirtless photos would end up on a postcard for "Curfew," a gay party that took place at a nightclub in NYC. I forget the club's name—maybe it was Tunnel.

I had actually been to the club once before college—but there are no pictures of me from that night. When I was a pre-freshman checking out NYU, the university assigned me to a student host to show me around the campus and the city.

I forgot his name, but he was a Puerto Rican kid—so, of course, the recruiters knew we would hit it off. I mean, weren't we all named "Luis Perez?"

He's the one who brought me to Curfew. Half the club was taken over for gay night. The other half for the straights. We were both underage, but—and this was the secret—they didn't card over at the gay party.

So we entered on the wild side without having to show ID and then crossed over into the hetero section of the dance floor.

You couldn't really tell the difference. The whole place looked pretty gay to me. So, of course, the music was great.

At one point I sat down and a kind Black man in a tight skirt and dark wig asked me if I was okay. *Because if you're not dancing, there must be something wrong.*

Later that night (early morning), my guide and I were eating in the twenty-four-hour McDonald's on West 3rd Street in the Village when we watched a huge Black dude beat the shit out of two drunk kids in their twenties.

It all started when one of the victims—a white kid—made the mistake of trying to rap in front of the Black man. The kid went down with one cheap shot. And then his Asian friend made the grave error of trying to reason with the Black man who had just KO'd his rhyming buddy. His face got busted open for that.

Apparently, the Black guy was in the right though, because everyone in the place—except for me and my paisano—was applauding the beatdown. Some customers even managed to get their own licks in on the bloodied kids before they stumbled out into the street to safety. This was peak World Star *before* World Star.

That night of deviance, violence, and danger won me over to NYU. Well, that night and the academic scholarship the College of Arts and Science gave me.

The city felt like a place where you could be whatever you wanted to be. Create your own Curfew. For me, my self-realization started with improv comedy—a group called Camp Anawanna Swim Team—and later sketch comedy with the Wicked Wicked Hammerkatz.

I never pursued an unpaid modeling career. I pursued an unpaid comedy career.

Such a shame. Back in the day somebody with connections would definitely have paid to watch me masturbate!

But today?

Today I'd have to be the one paying to watch.

LATINX

I wonder how my pre-frosh host is doing. Now in his early forties, is he still clubbing? I'm sure he's still Puerto Rican—but how does he identify?

If he's getting the NYU Latino Alumni Network newsletter like I am, then he may have noticed out of nowhere its name changed to the NYU *Latinx* Alumni Network (emphasis mine).

The first time I remember seeing it was back in 2018. And whatever latent Latin pride I had inside me came out.

What the fuck did you call me? I thought, staring down my inbox.

Latinx?

Was this a typo? A prank? Just an NYU thing?

Because when I hear "Latinx," I think of a Latino who is incapable of seducing your wife.

> *Sir, you don't have to worry about your*
> *pretty wife when hiring these landscapers.*
> *They're Latinx.*

At the time I didn't know any Latinos who identified as Latinx—I still don't know any. Something like 97 percent (on the low end) don't see themselves that way. And more than most have never even heard the word.

I bet more Latinos and Hispanics identity with "spic" than with Latinx. Personally, I find the ethnic slur preferable.

I recently learned that "Hispanic"—which I've always used interchangeably with Latin—was concocted not too long ago.

That's according to G. Cristina Mora in *Making Hispanics: How Activists, Bureaucrats, and Media Constructed a New American.* And thank you, University of Chicago Press, for putting the book's summary on your website:

> During the 1960 census, reports classified Latin American immigrants as "white," grouping them with European Americans. Not only was this decision controversial, but also Latino activists claimed that this classification hindered their ability to portray their constituents as underrepresented minorities. Therefore, they called for a separate classification: Hispanic.

For me, one difference between "Hispanic" and "Latinx" is that Hispanic feels like it came from within the group (and it did), whereas Latinx feels like it came from outside the group (even though, technically, it came from a very small minority within it).

Since 2018, I've been seeing Latinx forced into headlines, think pieces, and minds. What's clear from its ongoing marketing campaign is that it is easier to coerce progressive white people into using Latinx than it is to persuade Latinos to use it.

According to the abstract of a study titled *Who Identifies as "Latinx"? The Generational Politics of Ethnoracial Labels*, Mora and her coauthors conclude that "our findings show that 'Latinx' is largely understood as complementary to, not mutually exclusive of, other panethnic [sic] labels like 'Hispanic' and 'Latino.'" But that is among the Hispanics and Latinos they surveyed.

When it comes to the way non-Hispanic and non-Latinos use the word, Latinx has become mutually exclusive to the other labels. That's why every time "Latinx" is uttered, a woke angel gets its NPR tote bag.

But the term is still problematic. As Giancarlo Sopo put it in an op-ed for *USA Today*, "as the son of immigrants who grew up in a community with 'English-only' ordinances, I am among the many Americans who consider it an absurd Anglicization of a language that generations struggled to conserve."

Later in the same piece, Sopo goes on to write:

> Liberals should also realize it is impossible to reconcile their professed values—like multiculturalism, education and pronoun autonomy—with the peculiar strain of 2019 progressivism that seeks to radically change our language, disregards linguistic practices, *and disavows our right to determine how we are described* (emphasis mine).

There is an irony to the current warping of the English language, where supposedly inclusive words like Latinx—nonbinary plus Latin—end up being both exclusionary and nonconsensual.

The strain of 2019 progressivism Sopo describes has continued. There are more variants now—each one as annoying and hilarious as the others.

I remember a *Vice* headline from 2019: "What Happens When Latinx People Gentrify Latinx Communities."

At the time I thought a more appropriate headline would have been "What Happens When Latinx People Gentrify *Latino* Communities."

Because with only 3 percent of Latinos and Hispanics identifying as Latinx, what community are they even talking about? Is three Latinx roommates living in an apartment considered a "community" or the premise to a shitty dramedy?

If any gentrification is happening it is within the borders of *Vice*'s style guide, which dictates that the article be littered with Latin-*equis*.

The article deals with Boyle Heights in Los Angeles specifically, where residents make life miserable for any outsider looking to develop a business or even an art center in the Chicano neighborhood.

Boyle Heights xenophobes are fantastic! They are all about open borders when it comes to the United States—"Make America *Mexico* Again!"—but they go all in on "Build the Wall" around their 6.5 square miles of turf to keep out would-be settlers.

"Typically, the progenitors of gentrification are white," the article reads, "but what about when they're not?"

When America sends its people to Boyle Heights, they are…sending their best.

And Boyle Heights doesn't want them—whether they be white gentrifiers or *los gentefiers*—you know, the kinds of college-educated Latinos who have heard the word Latinx before and love improv comedy.

Thankfully I didn't have to take on student-loan debt to learn the word. And I can unsubscribe from my Latinx alumni newsletter at any time. Like nearly all Latinos and Hispanics, I never subscribed to it in the first place.

IN THE LOWS

I get this creeping feeling that embracing the woke will never be enough.

Just look at Lin-Manuel Miranda. Here we have the *Borinquen* musical theater god, whose *Hamilton* revolutionized Broadway. Miranda set the founding of the United States to hip-hop, made the Founding Fathers Black and brown rappers, and ultimately kept Harriet Tubman off the ten-dollar bill!

I got to see *Hamilton* live in New York City and it blew me away. My friend Sameer reminded me that years before I got to experience the musical in person, he played the original cast recording for me on our drive back from an open mic in Los Angeles—and I made fun of it.

He quotes me as saying, "This is so fucking corny!"

"*Hamilton* is hip-hop for people who don't really like hip-hop," Sameer said. "And show tunes for people who hate show tunes."

What can I say? My ability to appreciate corny things has grown over the years.

Although I still think Miranda should have written a scene where Hamilton's slaves teach him to rap. I think it would have helped the plot and lend some more historical accuracy to the production.

The winner of eleven Tony Awards was a masterpiece nonetheless and it looked like Miranda could do no wrong. But then he had to go and produce a film adaptation of his pre-*Hamilton* musical, *In the Heights.*

If you read the woke periodicals, the problem with *In the Heights* is that although the story takes place in the Dominican stronghold of Washington Heights, the Latinx leads are too light-skinned and the darker-skinned cast members might as well be Latin-xtras.

As a headline in *Vox* put it, "*In the Heights* exemplified the ugly colorism I've experienced in Latinx communities." The author of the article, Jasmine Haywood, explains:

> For a film set in a heavily Afro-Latinx neighborhood, darker-skinned people were relegated to dancers, hair salon workers, and other background roles. And among the leading roles, there was a glaring lack of Afro-Latinx representation.

First off, thank God Lin-Manuel didn't set the play in Boyle Heights—*In the Boyle Heights* would have been a mortal sin. The Chicano resistance fighters of BH wouldn't stand for it. Plus, how do you make a musical today where the good guys are the gentrifiers?

Second, I wonder how many of the actors who made it into the cast of *In the Heights* are even from Washington

Heights to begin with. I imagine a truly equitable casting process would have started on the streets of the neighborhood itself.

Picture Lin-Manuel holding auditions on Dyckman Street—approaching the Dominican men playing dominoes on the sidewalk. The darker ones, of course.

"*Papí,*" Lin-Manuel says. "Can you turn down your radio?"

With the *bachata* now barely audible, Lin-Manuel continues. "Sing me a few bars from *Hello, Dolly!* Then I'd like to see you do something from your favorite Bob Fosse number."

C'mon—I don't know how authentic musical theater is in the DR. But, as Haywood points out, colorism is a real thing in that community.

That's why whenever I have to play a racist character I no longer put on a Southern accent. Because the most racist people I've met are Dominicans.

Imagine hearing this in a thick Dominican accent: "Why did Rosa Parks ride the bus? Because she too lazy *to drive* the bus!"

Of course Lin-Manuel apologized via social media for his antiwoke sin. It was unintentional. After all, he "started writing *In The Heights* because I didn't feel seen. And over the past 20 years all I wanted was for us—ALL of us—to feel seen."

In his apology though, he addresses Afro-*Latinos* in particular. No mention of the Latinx—Afro or otherwise. It's a misstep that seems to have gone unnoticed.

Part of me can't believe he would apologize for any of this. I mean, he has all that *Hamilton* money—millions of literal Hamiltons. Now that's some Fuck-You money right there! More than enough to speak your mind and produce your projects your way.

One of my problems is that I've gotten ahead of myself: I've been saying "Fuck you" without "Fuck-You money."

But another part of me totally gets where his apology is coming from.

See, back in 2017 Lin-Manuel gave convicted Puerto Rican terrorist Oscar López Rivera a ticket to *Hamilton* in Chicago (the city—not some kind of play within a play).

The bombs that Rivera's Fuerzas Armadas de Liberación Nacional Puertorriqueña (FALN) detonated in the United States, the innocent people murdered and bodies maimed may not have won Puerto Rico its independence from the United States—but they did get Rivera a date with the Broadway star courtside at the hottest show in any town.

Thirty-five years behind bars, commuted sentence by President Obama, and tickets to *Hamilton*—not a bad deal overall.

Lin-Manuel has never apologized for it either. Why would he? In his community, colorism is a sin—but wining and dining a convicted terrorist of the Left is not. One act gets you written up by the woke scolds at *Vox*—the other gets a musical theater kid some street cred.

Miranda closes out his *In the Heights* apology with a promise: "I promise to do better in my future projects, and I'm dedicated to the learning and evolving we all have to do to make sure we are honoring our diverse and vibrant community."

To that end I think Lin-Manuel should issue at least a partial apology. Because rather than give a *Hamilton* ticket to an Afro-Latinx terrorist, he chose to give one to Oscar López Rivera—which is just more ugly colorism at play!

Concerned comrades might say, "At least hook up some Black Panthers with tickets to *Jagged Little Pill*."

BLACK CARTOONS, BLACK VOICES[29]

The top three roles that have defined my acting career: the Troll in the *Three Billy Goats Gruff* (1st grade), George Washington (5th grade), and the voice of Hero in a McDonald's commercial (years after getting my MFA).

A handsome Latin race car driver—think of me, but thinner and better-looking—enters a Mickey D's franchise. His name is Hero and I am the voice in Hero's head—his voice! He looks the way he's supposed to look and I sound the way he's supposed to sound.

Hero moves through commercial life like a man who enjoys the sound of his own voice—the only voice he can trust. As he walks to the register—with Formula One grace, not NASCAR brutality—I recount for him the race he obviously just won. Post-champagne shower, he has

---

29 A version of this chapter was first published in *Spiked* as "Can only black people voice black cartoon characters?"

earned whatever combo meal the McDonald's campaign was promoting that month.

The voice I put on?

Think Antonio Banderas—but with a circumcised ponytail. Hear him speak these words: *cruising, track, Big Mac, chicken nuggets....*

Goddamn—I made a lot of money on that spot! And for only a few hours of work, most of it spent on the drive over to the studio—which is part of the magic of voiceover.

I have never gotten the opportunity to voice Hero again. You can say I was canceled the old-fashioned way, without any public-relations uproar—I just wasn't hired again.

Some actors, eager to remain on the right side of whatever history is being made up today, have even started to preemptively cancel themselves.

After twenty years of voicing the Cleveland Brown character on *Family Guy*, Mike Henry gave up the role. What is obvious now—but was not twenty years ago or even twenty minutes before the VO artist's announcement hit social media—is that "persons of color should play characters of color."

Henry is not a person of color, but Cleveland is a character of color, so Henry handed in his tweet of resignation.

At the time this was trending my guess was that the show would have to find an actor of color—in this case, a Black one—who could perform the voice Henry had created for the beloved Cleveland. And so they did, hiring a talented impressionist and YouTube star named Arif Zahir to fill the role. Although Zahir is much younger than the cartoon character he's voicing and his skin tone isn't *exactly* Cleveland Brown's brown (Zahir's complexion fluctuates depending on the lighting in his YouTube videos) the guy's Cleveland impression is flawless.

Unfortunately, the same can't be said for Kevin Michael Richardson's Dr. Hibbert on *The Simpsons*, who for thirty years was voiced by Harry Shearer. Though Richardson is a talented voice actor—and, most importantly in these times, a Black voice actor—the change just doesn't work. But it looks like it's going to be permanent. Because as *The New York Times* reported, the producers of *The Simpsons* made it official company policy to "'no longer have white actors voice nonwhite characters.'"

Fine.

But if you're going to make the cartoon equivalent of a cover band at least make sure the singer sounds like the original. I'm sure there are plenty of hungry YouTubers out there who can nail the Hibbert chuckle.

And if you can't find one, well, there's no harm in killing off the character entirely. Dr. Hibbert may be Black, but he is fictional. No one will take to the streets over the death of Springfield's jolly physician—or the demise of any of the other eight-fingered, nonyellow characters-of-color on the show.

Perhaps the producers of *Family Guy* will have to give the Cleveland treatment to the other cartoon characters Mike Henry voiced, like Consuela the Hispanic maid, and any others that check the POC box on the actor's IMDb page.

(Dear FOX: Should the role of Consuela need filling, I may not have the voice you're looking for, but I do have the last name.)

When it comes to abdicating animated roles, Mike Henry and Harry Shearer are not alone. Most notable is probably *The Simpsons'* legend Hank Azaria. (I'll dedicate some pages to Azaria later.) There is also Alison Brie, who wishes she hadn't voiced Diane Nguyen on *BoJack Horseman*: "I now understand that people of color, [sic] should always voice people of color." (Sounds familiar.) And Kristen Bell, who gave up voicing a mixed-race character in *Central Park*.

But wait, men will still voice some of the show's women characters. Because race is immutable, but biological sex is not? I guess for the time being that's where we're following the science to.

With Hollywood and activism, it's easy to be cynical. The problem with casting actors for videos like the #ITakeResponsibility one from 2020 is that it always comes off like they're acting.

In case you don't remember, *I Take Responsibility* is the short black-and-white video that features white actors like Julianne Moore, Debra Messing, and Jesse Pinkman looking into their iPhone cameras and "taking responsibility" for… *systemic racism*?

I don't know. Some of the lines they deliver sound like forced confessions. I mean, does the star of *Will & Grace* really believe she has the blood of Black Americans on her hands? (Shit, what does the rest of her sitcom cast think about that?)

Other lines from the video read like general warnings. For example, you better not make any racist jokes around Stanley Tucci from now on. See, the Tooch went sixty years on this planet allowing "racist, hurtful words" to be uttered in his presence—but the script he's reading off of makes it clear that injustice ends now! I'm sure the bravery of the bald star of *The Hunger Games* franchise and *Undercover Blues* is sure to trickle down into the streets.

Even Kristen Bell makes a cameo in the cringe-inducing PSA. She's playing her nonmixed-race self this time around, so it's totally cool now, you know.

This NAACP-approved video and the animation casting bow-outs happened around the same time Black Lives Matter protests were erupting across the country. So, many will brush off woke moves like Brie's, Bell's, and Henry's as virtue-signaling/career insurance. *You know, they're just trying to live to work another day in Hollywood.*

But I believe many actors and actresses are acting in good faith. They want to be good. They want to do good. And as good allies they will use whatever platforms they have to achieve that. That may mean removing oneself from the recording booth and letting a person of color step to the mic.

Just imagine how many lives would have been saved if Harry Shearer had stepped down earlier from his place on *The Simpsons* and let George Floyd voice Dr. Hibbert....

Jenny Slate is doing her part too. She gave up playing the role of Missy Foreman-Greenwald on Netflix's *Big Mouth*. As the actress explained on Instagram:

> At the start of the show, I reasoned with myself that it was permissible for me to play 'Missy' because her mom is Jewish and white—as am I. But 'Missy' is also black, and black characters on an animated show should be played by black people.

Slate reasoned herself into the role and later out of the role. But the implications of her reasoning make me uncomfortable. Maybe this is my fragility showing, but it seems that in order "to engage in meaningful anti-racist action," as Slate wants to continue doing, you have to resurrect archaic views on race. When it comes to Missy, that means erasing the character's mixed identity and declaring her Black by some kind of cartoon version of the one-drop rule.

Slate apologized to "anyone that I've hurt." But I really can't imagine she hurt anybody. *Big Mouth* is a cartoon show where hormone monsters guide kids through the awkwardness of puberty and all that comes with it: excitement, shame, perversion. Pillows get pregnant in this world! The show's hilarious! (At least, the first three seasons were.)

Slate's statement reads more like the script of a recent convert to the faith. It's her own #ITakeResponsibility—but more meaningful. She seeks to atone for her white privilege—but antiracism will never forgive her for that, no matter how many promises she makes to do better. So she invents another sin for herself: making a cute voice for a fictional character "problematic."

Missy Foreman-Greenwald was more than her white Jewish mother and Black father and more than her brown skin. She was a lovable dork, romantic, and a pervert. She was a kid, voiced by an adult woman who looks nothing like her, but sounds exactly as she should—which is another part of the magic of voiceover. It's an art. Jenny Slate is an artist. (If you need a good palate cleanse watch or listen to her voice Marcel the Shell with Shoes On. Do it now. The next paragraph will still be here.)

Now, what *Big Mouth* loses with Slate's exit it hopes to make up for with her replacement, Ayo Edebiri, who is real full-on-Black to fictional Missy's half. It's that kind of racial essentialism the producers of the show and Netflix are comfortable with.

In addition to voicing Missy, Edebiri was also hired to be a writer on the show. So, fans who stick with the Netflix hit should ready themselves for storylines infused with that authentic Black experience of a daughter of Nigerian immigrants who grew up writing *Twilight* fan-fiction when she was supposed to be paying attention in Latin class, did improv comedy, and, when she speaks, happens to sound whiter than Jenny Slate. When you're a Black girl who dates white guys you have to worry about catching HPV and Brad's speech patterns.

What's ironic is that while Edebiri's voice doesn't do the part of Missy Foreman-Greenwald justice, her real-life bio does.

The code-switching storyline in "A Very Special 9-11 Episode" in season four was cute: Missy (still voiced by Slate), with the help of her Black friend DeVon, navigates how and when to change her speech (e.g., when to sound Black), depending on the race of the people she's interacting with. But, if we're being real, "code-switching" for the parties involved in *Big Mouth* is more like when the Black kid on your improv team who went to Swarthmore starts a scene talking like he went to Rutgers.

Can we get a one-word suggestion?

Equity!

So, I'm probably not going to tune in to seasons five and six to watch Missy on the rest of her journey through puberty and self-identity. But let me know when a white actor on *Big Mouth* steps down from voicing one of the kid's penises or vaginas on the show. Representation matters. The conversation on systemic racism continues. And it's about time white actors step aside to let people of color be dicks and pussies.

10

APU PROBLEMS[30]

At some point everyone stops watching *The Simpsons*. And yet it continues, producing new episodes that I, and no one I know, watch. It doesn't matter though. When it comes to *The Simpsons*, I don't matter. In the same way I don't matter to gravity or to the other forces of nature. *The Simpsons* will outlast gravity.

Nevertheless, the animated TV institution has attracted would-be assassins who hope to kill it—but have to settle for maiming it.

A few years back it looked like the show was going to kill off Apu Nahasapeemapetilon, its iconic but recently controversial, Indian-American character. (Apu became a naturalized citizen back in season seven.) This came after the release of activist-comedian Hari Kondabolu's documentary, *The Problem with Apu*, which claimed the shopkeeper character, voiced by Hank Azaria, is a racist stereotype.

---

30 A version of this chapter was first published in *Spiked* as "The problem with Apu's critics."

Why stop there? I thought. If the show's cartoon depiction of Kwik-E-Mart owner Apu was a slap in the face to sensitive Indian-Americans like Kondabolu, then the show's treatment of Bumblebee Man was a kick to the nuts of my people…Hispanics who dress like bumblebees.

So I went ahead and strapped on my wings and antennae and produced a documentary of my own with the help of bumblebee allies to address the lasting, racist legacy of *The Simpsons'* Bumblebee Man.

I wasn't born an activist. But I had no choice but to become one after I watched Kondabolu's documentary—which assured me that it is okay for a grown man to be angry at a cartoon.

Man, the responses to *The Problem with Bumblebee Man* were amazing! In particular the people who watched it and thought it was legit and not a parody.

I mean, c'mon! There's a scene in it where my character (dressed in his bee getup) is trying to commiserate with a bumblebee furry about the daily struggles of our *abeja* people—but it turns out my comrade isn't interested in the cause. He just wants to fuck another guy in a bee costume.

There were many *Simpsons* apologists who took to the comments sections of YouTube and Facebook to let me know that the Bumblebee Man was in fact a parody of *El Chapulín Colorado* (The Red Grasshopper), a character from a Mexican comedy series that ran in the 1970s—so I shouldn't be offended.

I guess we Hispanics who dress like bumblebees and grasshoppers all look the same, huh? And we should just shut our mandibles and proboscises….

Yeah, I had a lot of fun leaning into the whole bit.

While I mock Hari's crusade against a cartoon, the two of us actually have some things in common. We both self-identify as comedians, we're both from Queens, New York, and my father—like both of Hari's parents—is an immigrant. Albeit my dad's from Argentina—where cows aren't worshipped, but beef is.

So while I was called lots of things on the proverbial playground—like "Julio" and "Ricardo," "Lopez" and "spic"—I was never called "Apu." Although I imagine the kids who called Hari "Apu" were rather diverse, with Queens being the mixed borough that it is. Diversity is our strength—even if it extends to bullies.

Like Apu—a father of eight—my dad to five boys has a "funny" accent too. Think of The Most Interesting Man in the World from those Dos Equis commercials, but gruffer and with a more limited English vocabulary. For those meeting him for the first time (or even after several times) he can be hard to understand. I'm basically bilingual—in that I speak English and I speak my dad's version of English. Not only can it be funny, but it is also a reminder of my roots. I even like hearing others try to put on my dad's accent.

Now my mother's accent is just as thick as my dad's—but from Queens. (Members of her tribe pronounce toilet as "turlette"—which should be the correct pronunciation anyway.)

Like Hari, I talk about my folks on stage too. I have one stand-up bit where I lament my parents' accents—not because I'm embarrassed for them, but because I know how much they love each other. But unfortunately their accents are so thick they limit what kinds of sexual role-playing they can do.

After nearly forty years of marriage I know they want to spice things up—and my dad wants to play off-type, to challenge himself as a performer in the bedroom. The swarthy *Tucumano* may have become an American citizen— but he still has that immigrant work ethic and Latin lust. (*Papi's* no Latinx.)

Like, Dad wants to play Mom's high school science teacher—she hasn't turned in her homework assignment!— but he ends up cast as the school janitor instead. (He may have the keys to the lab room but no lesson plan.)

Dad buys a seersucker suit and whip to play a plantation master in the antebellum South—Mom, the slave girl, who hasn't turned in her slave work!—but he ends up putting away the costume and prop whip, forced instead to play some migrant worker Mom picks up outside a Home Depot. (He'll tend to her garden—after they haggle over the price— and Mom threatens to call ICE on him. But it's a *sexy threat*, of course.)

It sucks—these casting woes. I imagine their default role-play is the one where my father is the victim of a hate crime on Long Island and Mom plays the perpetrator's mother.

This may be why my favorite moment in *The Problem with Apu* is when, right after Hari comments on how ridiculous Hank Azaria's Indian accent is, we meet Hari's parents for the first time.

I swear I am not thinking about them fucking. (But now you are...I'm sure Hari's Indian *padres* have to deal with their own type-casting in the bedroom.)

No, parental erotic fan-fiction aside, what I love about that moment in the documentary is that Hari's parents... kinda sound like Apu.

They. Do.

Now if *I* had produced *The Problem with Apu*—it'd be rated X!—and if my thesis still rested heavily on the idea that "*Nobody. Sounds. Like. Apu.*"—I would make sure *nobody* in the doc sounds like Apu.

No stereotypical accents allowed anywhere near the set! I don't care if they're Hari's parents. Either recast them for some first-generation Indian-Americans from Berkeley or leave them out of the picture entirely. Pretend Hari's an orphan. Yeah, get that orphan sympathy! (Have you seen *Lion*? Dev Patel. Beautiful. Tear fest.... Wish we could cast Dev Patel to play Hari!)

But if the star insists on keeping his parents—for "authenticity" purposes or whatever—fine. But take away all their lines. They're not helping. I'm thinking whenever we check in on them they're staged in *tableau*. Anything to do the narrative (social) justice!

I watched a video on YouTube where the channel Asian Boss took to the streets of Mumbai to film "Indians React to Apu Controversy." There are a range of reactions the *Indian*-Indians in that video have to clips of Apu. Some find the character funny. Others find him hacky and outdated. Some even find him offensive. But what all the man-on-the-street interviewees have in common is—just like Hari's parents—they too kinda sound like Apu. Especially the ones who deny it.

It's rather damning. I mean, if the sample size of that video is any indication, apparently a billion people on the Indian subcontinent speak English somewhere on the Apu spectrum.

To be clear: I am not saying this as a putdown.

I wonder, why is there so much shame attached to this stereotypical Indian accent?

If I were to put on a stereotypical French accent that would be totally fine. It might even be considered sexy. (If my dad could do a French accent imagine what fun he and my mom could have in their love dojo!)

But for some reason if you sound like a telecom operator who says his name is "John Smith" but is really "Sameer Singh" or you sound like the guy working the register at a real-life Kwik-E-Mart, that's something to be ashamed of?

Just think of all the Indian gurus who've seduced western women over the years. Yoga, the third eye, enlightenment—sure. But when it comes time to seal the deal with some *Eat, Pray, Love*, the yogi knows what to do: lay that sweet Apu accent on thick. *Thank you, come again.* (My dad has no chance of doing that.)

I'm sure there's a B-minus college paper in here somewhere. Something like "Deconstructing the Post-Colonial Structural Hegemony of 'Cool' Accents."

One could even bust out a few paragraphs on how Hari Kondabolu should have been decolonizing the American accent—Apu'ing the fuck out of it!—but instead he was guilty of complicity: helping to colonize it through assimilation and erasure. (Some kid will go into debt to write this college paper.)

* * *

Hari was criticized for leaving out interviews he had done with Indian-American small-business owners. As Amar Shah, who refers to himself on Twitter as "Son of the Real Apu," pointed out, "Everybody has an opinion about Apu, but did they ever talk to someone who owned a convenience store or gas station or work in one or grow up in one? You know, like my dad and I?"

Shah likened Apu to his real-life father—in a good way—and shared stories of pride and love for his old man. Reading that Twitter thread of his I couldn't help but think of my own dad and the similar tales I could tell about him and our family's butcher shop in Spanish Harlem.

On *The Lou Perez Podcast*, I spoke with Ankit Shukla, author of the book *I Love You, APU*, about his own family's immigrant experience, which includes owning a convenience store in the US (while Indian), and his attempt to reach out to Hari to talk about Hari's *problem* and Ankit's *love* of Apu. (According to Ankit, that conversation never happened. Hari blocked him on Twitter.)

Hari says the interviews with those working-class Indians had to be cut for time. That may be true. But I'm betting they were cut because the working-class immigrants he spoke to didn't care about Apu—some probably sounded like Apu too—and they had more pressing matters on their minds.

Ask yourself this: Would Apu give a shit about Apu?

But, more than that, I think the fact that Indian immigrants continue to own and operate convenience stores is an uncomfortable truth for classists like Hari. Instead of featuring real-life people who perpetuate the Kwik-E-Mart stereotype, Hari would rather populate his documentary with "respectable" Indian-Americans who work in showbiz—and complain about their lack of representation in showbiz.

An article on Wisconsin Public Radio's website describes Hari as an "iconoclast" who "speaks truth to power." I guess sometimes speaking truth to power means hiding the icky side of the truth and erasing the powerless from the final cut.

* * *

When it was looking like Apu would be no more, Hari was upset. He lamented the news of Apu's departure, tweeting, "There are so many ways to make Apu work without getting rid of him. If true, this sucks."

Look, you can't make a documentary in which you liken *The Simpsons* to a "racist grandfather," accuse the white guy voicing a character you dislike of committing "cultural appropriation" at best or doing a minstrel show at worst, and then act shocked when the show's producers contemplate killing off the problematic character.

Something else worth mentioning: In the doc, Hari cites the attacks of September 11, 2001, as the catalyst that put him on this hero's journey of his. To really drive the point home, the filmmaker goes so far as to incorporate a cheap visual effect: Hari is facing the camera and in the lenses of his eyeglasses the viewer is shown footage of the Twin Towers engulfed in flames. It comes out of nowhere and is more gross than my summary of it.

(For my parody I wish I had photoshopped bee wings to The Falling Man!)

* * *

There is a Hamletian moment at the end of my mockumentary parody. Our Hispanic Bumblebee asks: "Am I just humorless, overly sensitive, and petty? Am I riding fashionable social-justice causes to put myself in the spotlight, while assassinating the work of better artists who have made millions of people laugh?"

Of course he is! That's where we are right now, baby!

* * *

Whatever happens with his career, Hari may never find closure with the cartoon that hurt him. Because Apu may or may not be on the way out. In an interview for *USA Today* marking 700 episodes of *The Simpsons*, creator Matt Groening said they are "working on something kind of ambitious" for the character.

Whatever that is it won't involve Hank Azaria voicing him (or any white actors voicing any of the nonwhite—I mean, nonyellow—characters from now on).

Although Hari wasn't able to get Azaria to appear in *The Problem with Apu*—and there's a scene in the doc of Hari's poorly acted indignation for being turned down by the actor—Azaria has come around to apologize for the harm he caused. In fact, the legendary voice actor wants to "apologize to every single Indian person" for voicing Apu.

That Hank Azaria Yom Kippur group text is going to be epic!

But after he sends it out, I think it's only fair that all the Indians who sound like Apu apologize too.[31]

It was during an episode of the *Armchair Expert* podcast where Azaria went deep and confessed his sins—among them, his participation in structural racism—to hosts Dax Shepard and Monica Padman.

It's a painful hour and a half to get through. Both Azaria and Shepard are in recovery and seem to feel just as much guilt for being white as they do for being addicts. Their drug addictions hurt those close to them. Their whiteness hurt the universe.

Monica Padman being there is very on-the-nose—the Indian girl who grew up in Georgia (the state, not the

---

31   TikTok deemed this joke hate speech.

country) standing in to represent all Indians. Thankfully they call it out on the episode. They even have a laugh about it. She is the co-host after all, but ironically it's easy to forget she's even there, as the two successful white guys hog the mic and more than once explain how Padman—the brown, "marginalized," "person of color"—is made to feel day in and day out because of white guys like them.

Between commercials for HelloFresh, Squarespace, and MasterClass there is lots of talk of "white fragility" and "white privilege," an accounting of the tremendous toll racism takes on white people's humanity and compassion; "Latinx" gets a shoutout; "Defund the Police" gets an apologia; and Azaria is now doing "equity" work for some organization called the Soul Focused Group—not to be confused with the equity work he does as a member of the SAG-AFTRA union.

* * *

Now I'm not in recovery, but I know that one of the steps in Alcoholics Anonymous is to let go of the things you can't control (like your addiction) and trust in a higher power. That's a big ask to begin with. And I'm afraid addicts looking for help are going to listen to this episode of *Armchair Expert* and come away thinking sobriety just isn't worth trusting in the higher power of a woke god.

When I turned off the episode, I know I needed a drink.

(Good news though: whether you continue to use or go sober you can still get twenty-five dollars off from Brooklinen if you use the promo code "expert.")

* * *

Looking back, the one good thing about the whole Apu controversy is that it's brought a lot of love the show's way too. Whereas Hari and Azaria see Apu as a bad Indian stereotype, others have paid tribute to him and reminded us of the many things we loved most about the character.

Apu is a testament to the brilliance of *The Simpsons*, whose writers bring depth to so many two-dimensional figures by playing with stereotypes and by transcending them. In his interview with *USA Today*, Groening said he's proud of Apu. And he's right to be. Apu brought a lot of joy into the world.

The simple truth is this: it is far easier to destroy Apu than it is to create him. Too bad we had to destroy him to find that out.

11

CREMATION VACATION

To celebrate turning thirty-three, my friend Rob and I decided to take a trip together. It would be our first ever—and without our girlfriends. While we could have gone to Vegas or New Orleans for our birthdays, Rob thought it would be special to spend the opening days of our Jesus years on a pilgrimage of sorts and go somewhere we never would have expected to go.

So we booked our flights for Nepal for February 2015. Before I had even packed I was already generating material from the trip. Imagining the tagline for a feature film: "Two bros from Queens looking to show the Third World how to party!"

While I was asking another well-traveled friend of mine if he knew of any comedy clubs in Kathmandu that I might be able to get up at—he did not—Rob was researching Buddhist and Hindu temples and coming up with our agenda. It was more of a spiritual journey for my friend—but I was happy to tag along.

We both loved Eddie Murphy's *The Golden Child*—and some of its most memorable scenes take place in Kathmandu. Maybe there was a *Golden Child* guided tour? (But it turns out those scenes weren't shot on location. They were done on a soundstage back in Hollywood. You don't have to look too hard to tell: It's supposed to be freezing in Nepal, but you can't see any of the actors' breath.)

It was ten hours to Istanbul from the JFK Airport, a three-hour layover, then six hours more to Kathmandu. When we arrived, we slipped into the backseat of a cab no bigger than a go-cart and were driven dangerously through poverty like I had never seen to check in to a hotel Rob had booked for us through Expedia.

The alleyway we had to squeeze through to get to the entrance of the hotel gave the place away. I have no idea where they got the pictures they posted online. But their fraud worked—it got us foreigners through the narrow door.

The place had Wi-Fi—but no hot water for the shower. Each morning they were going to give us a bucket of warm water to wash up. And we would have to share the bathroom (not sure about the bucket) with two other rooms. I stared at a grapefruit-sized hole in the bathroom floor that we were supposed to wash ourselves over and, if we had to go, squat over too.

Back in the room Rob pointed to a bowl of plastic fruit that lay on a stool. "Even the plastic fruit is rotten," he said. And it was.

The room was not worth the fifteen dollars a night. We checked out—but paid for it in full—then took another bumpy go-cart cab ride over to the Hotel Yak & Yeti— appropriate contemporary lodging for two divas like us.

The Yak & Yeti complex was gated with security detail meeting our cab at the entrance. There were Buddhist monks walking through the halls of the hotel. I couldn't tell if they were guests or staff members in costume—like the Siddhartha Gautama version of a Jekyll and Hyde-themed restaurant. Outside on the building's grounds was a small lake with real swans and ducks.

The Nepalese were very kind people, which made it uncomfortable watching the Indian guests at the hotel speaking down to the staff and ordering them around like they were of a lower caste. (Perhaps technically they were.)

"Don't talk to him like that!" I wanted to say. "We're white—that's supposed to be our thing."

Rob and I spent our time visiting centuries-old temples, drinking beer, and eating Nepali momos (dumplings). Traffic mayhem aside, it was a very chill vacation.

One day we visited the sacred Hindu Pashupatinath Temple. In addition to tourists and the faithful, the temple was packed with wandering Hindu holy men called *Sadhus*.

Our tour guide told us that Sadhus take a vow of poverty and abstain from sex and alcohol. But they're allowed to smoke and drink this kind of cannabis concoction.

So they don't work and they're high all day, I thought. *Sadhus are pretty much your college roommate.*

Rob and I paid to have our pictures taken with two Sadhus: long hair, long beards, painted faces, and bright garments. We later learned that the more made-up a Sadhu is the more likely he's a conman, playing the role to take tourists' money. Just like Elmo does in Times Square.

The real hard core Sadhus are easier to spot though, because in addition to asceticism they take a vow of nudity. And they don't want to be filmed.

The two major warnings our guide gave us were not to film the holy men and not to make eye contact with the monkeys that hang around the temple. They are very aggressive and will rob you. The monkeys, that is.

We spent time at the Basmeshowr Ghat, which is the complex's crematorium. Bodies are burned in the open air on the banks of the Bagmati River and eventually the ashes are dumped into the water.

I look away from a burning body and see a monkey. Before I can make eye contact with the monkey, I look away, but then I'm staring at another burning body....

The day wasn't particularly windy, but we were definitely breathing in the smoke of the dead. It was a moving experience, being so close to these funeral pyres, surrounded by grieving strangers, and yet we were all sharing in the convergence of life and death—at the mercy of thuggish monkeys....

We're supposed to be on vacation, I thought. *I don't want to be thinking about my mortality.*

I turned away from a burning body to see dick. A lot of dick. Well, a lot of naked holy men, lazing around with their shriveled dicks exposed to the sun.

Not one guy had a nice piece. I imagine a vow of celibacy can do that to a man. Use it or lose it, you know.

A group of naked Sadhus was passing around a joint. Watching it slip between their dirty lips, I'd prefer inhaling the fumes of the dead.

I started to think, maybe these guys don't take a vow of nudity. Maybe they're just too stoned to put on clothes.

A small crowd gathers around one naked Sadhu who manages to stand up, even though he's high. I make eye-contact with him—my mistake—and he calls me over to him.

He points to a big stone sitting on the ground in front of him. He doesn't speak English, but manages to communicate with me.

"Lift it," he says, without words.

Whenever the opportunity is there for me to make a fool out of myself, Rob encourages me to do so. He's been doing it ever since high school.

So, I try to lift the stone—but I can't. It's too heavy. Then I think, *Okay, I get it—I'm that tourist now.*

The Sadhu responds to my weakness by telling me through pantomime that if I pay him, he will lift the stone with his penis.

And to show me and all those in attendance that he's serious, he kind of unravels his penis. Like, this is what he'd be working with—if he could get hard.

Now this is something I would normally pay to see—a man lift a rock with his cock. Honestly I'd pay to watch a man lift anything with his dick—it doesn't have to be a rock. Just as long as I don't have to spot him.

But then I thought, *Maybe this isn't the appropriate place for a man to be lifting things with his schlong? You know—with all the burning bodies and grieving widows hanging around? It's not exactly a bachelorette party.*

Plus, the guy wanted one hundred dollars.

I wasn't going to pay one hundred dollars for some dick! Something I could probably see for free online. So I waved my hands: "No thanks, holy man."

Rob and I left the temple and got into another go-cart cab, but by this time in the trip we were used to driving through Kathmandu. And by this time I was already regretting not paying the Sadhu to watch him lift that stone with his penis. Because even surrounded by all that death and poverty we still had the opportunity to share a few laughs.

Besides, I bet if I haggled with him I could have gotten him down to something reasonable, like twenty bucks.

Two months after our trip, Nepal suffered a catastrophic earthquake. Many of the places we visited were destroyed. What was especially eerie was that Rob had gotten a tattoo of one of the temples just before it was gone from the Earth.

I organized a couple benefit shows in Los Angeles, where I was living at the time. One show at my home club, Echoes Under Sunset, and the other in a space at the Upright Citizens Brigade Theatre Sunset.

Between the two shows—where I did my Nepal material—I think I raised something like two hundred dollars. The equivalent of a naked holy man lifting a rock with his penis twice.

I don't know where the money I raised ever went—I never audited the Red Cross—but I knew the Nepalese were going to rebuild their homes and their holy sites with whatever they got. Even if that meant enlisting high holy men to move the rubble with their penises.

12

D.I.E.

Do we have what it takes to create an industry, let alone a world, that is truly diverse, inclusive, and equitable?

I am not talking about the will to bring about such changes. I'm talking about the populations needed to do so. Now I am by no means a demographer, but I've been crunching the numbers and I find the results troubling.

For example, when it comes to decolonizing improv and sketch comedy—which is a real thing activists are trying to do—"The goal...is to have BIPOC [that is Black, Indigenous People of Color] performers represented in the Groundlings at the same level that they are represented in the community at large. In L.A. County, for example, that would mean about 49 percent Latino, 15 percent Asian, 9 percent Black, and 2 percent American Indian, Natives Alaskan, or Native Hawaiian."

With 75 percent of the sketch and improv troupe reserved for BIPOCers, that would leave only 25 percent of slots available for white people—you know, the population most interested in the Groundlings.

Diversity-inclusion-and-equity revolutionaries may think their hearts are in the right place—ready to turn away talented ofays by the hundreds—but do you want to be the D.I.E representative who says, "No," to an American Indian with dreams of bringing laughter to the world because your 2-percent indigenous slot has already been filled?

(To wit: the theater's representation percentages would be totally upended if the Groundlings decided to move to, say Newport Beach, California, where it is over 80 percent white.)

In order to meet the 40 percent Latino quota in Los Angeles, the Groundlings will have to do a lot of outreach to the Chicano community—which will ultimately fail. You're not going to see diversity recruiters hitting the streets of Boyle Heights or cruising Home Depot parking lots for Mexican day laborers to improvise, develop sketch content, and audition for Montreal's *Just for Laughs* and *Saturday Night Live*. You know, what would basically be a live-action *South Park* episode, where instead of the boys hiring migrants to write their essays (like in the "Writing Eses" episode), they'll be hiring them to write submission packets for shows like *South Park*.

No, with all this talk of D.I.E.ing, recruiters still will be targeting Latinos like me: college-educated—I even got an MFA!—and who got into improv and sketch comedy because all of our friends are white. Sure, we have Spanish last names, but we're still comedy nerds. Just like Lin-Manuel Miranda— FALN-supporting Rican that he is—is still a musical theater dork. That's how these things go. You can't force interests onto people—to do so would reek of colonization.

Remember when it was announced that Malia Obama was going to be a writer on one of Donald Glover's projects—no one thought about all the other African-American Harvard graduates who weren't going to be writing on the show, because President Obama's daughter took their spot.[32] Malia may be fantastic though—after all both her mom and dad are gifted performers.

Fortunately for other Black female college grads—who are not the daughters of former US presidents—race-based opportunities abound. If you're anything but white, now is your time.

Back in 2020 *The L.A. Times* reported that CBS wanted "at least 40 percent of its writers to be Black, indigenous or people of color by the 2021–22 broadcast season and has earmarked 25 percent of its future script-development money to projects with BIPOC creators or producers" and "also set a goal for the 2022–23 broadcast season: Half of all writers will be nonwhite."

Questions about talent, experience, and connections aside, are there even enough nonwhite writers around to staff all these shows? Like, how many Indian parents are going to be okay with their first-generation American children pursuing comedy instead of traditionally noble professions?

If it turns out there aren't enough applicants, are we to expect BIPOC and POC's to work two or more staffing jobs at the same time just so corporate can hit its quotas?

---

32 In college, Donald and I were friends and members of NYU's Wicked Wicked Hammerkatz. Donald is the most talented person I have ever worked with, and I am in no position to question that man's career decisions. But what should be obvious is that a talent like his transcends whatever racial, ethnic, and gender categories you're trying to showcase and uplift. Donald Glovers—i.e., geniuses—are definitely underrepresented.

Unfortunately, this kind of ethnic bean counting is being implemented everywhere—in entertainment and beyond. Other industries are taking on similar equity goals. Remember when United Airlines set its own diversity target of "50 percent of Students at New Pilot Training Academy To Be Women and People of Color"?

Don't get me wrong—I think there is a lot of good that will come with having more women pilots, who, unlike their male counterparts, have no problem stopping to ask for directions. But I do worry that planes flown by Black men are more likely to be pulled over midair by police.

I am afraid that ditching meritocracy and even personal interest in exchange for woke virtue signaling discrimination is just not going to work out. How can it? Entertainment, airlines, and every other industry with D.I.E. hiring practices will be recruiting from the same pool of brown bodies. Even the CIA wants to see more diversity in espionage and toppling foreign governments. (Of course, I'm talking about the Central Intelligence Agency—not the Culinary Institute of America. Although the chef CIA does have a Diversity Council. Who knows what covert operations they're up to!)

There may come a day when a BIPOC trans woman is forced to be a CBS staff writer by day, moonlight as a pilot for United Airlines, and, when she's not being nominated for an Oscar (which implemented new "representation and inclusion standards...in the Best Picture category"), she's gathering intel on the latest drone strikes in Yemen.[33]

Girl, if you think your existence is exhausting now—just wait!

---

33   If you're a Yemenite and want Americans to give a shit about you, get into showbiz.

REAL WHITE CHICKS, FAKE BLACK WOMEN[34]

I'm old enough to remember when it was considered a noble goal for the United States to become a colorblind society. I'm also old enough to have forgotten when that goal of colorblindness became, you know, just another way to perpetuate systemic racism. I don't know how we got here, but I'm afraid I might be one of those perpetuators who "doesn't see color." Because, if I'm being real, lots of people of color look white to me.

Alexandria Ocasio-Cortez? White chick. And the definition of white privilege is when you can look like her boyfriend, Riley, and still date AOC. I guess one way for woke Latinas to fight colorism is to date men with no color.

Meghan Markle? White chick. But apparently the mother of the anti-monarch Duchess of Sussex is Black and

34   A version of this chapter was first published in *The Spectator's world edition* as "Borrowing Blackness."

her father white, which makes her 50 percent Black and 50 percent white. I'll just have to take their word for it. But judging by her public personae: she is 100 percent actress.

You know, I still remember when I found out Colin Kaepernick is Black—I was like, "Woah! This changes everything!" I couldn't tell from his pictures. Now whenever I see him on television I clutch my purse.

Since that revelation it's been interesting watching Kaep, the quarterback activist, grow (out his afro). When people aren't talking about the NFL's supposed collusion to keep him off the field—and not the offers from teams that he turned down—they're talking about Kaep's woke public musings. When he speaks it's like we're watching him learn US history in real time. You can always tell which Rage Against the Machine album he just listened to. When he called for the release of convicted cop killer Mumia Abu-Jamal, I figured he was up to Rage's *The Battle of Los Angeles*.

These old-timey Perez eyes of mine get it wrong *a lot*—but sometimes they're onto something.

Five years after Rachel Dolezal shocked the world with the revelation of her whiteness, we saw three back-to-back cases of white-women-pretending-to-be-Black go viral. And this was outside the world of voice acting! This all happened in the real world—3D, white flesh and blood. These sisters Daniel-Day-Lewis'd it and went all-in on their roles. If you want to see what commitment to a part looks like, keep reading.

Do you remember the case of Satchuel Paigelyn Cole? Cole was a community leader in Indianapolis who worked with groups like Black Lives Matter and Showing Up for Racial Justice.

While "Satch" had been a white chick her whole life, she hadn't always been named Satchuel. In 2010 she changed her name from Jennifer Lynn Benton to a mix of Satchel Paige, legendary pitcher of the Negro leagues, and Chantelle Owens-Cole, Benton's African-American friend.

The name combination sounds like Benton was trying to concoct a spell: Historical Black Figure + Black Woman I Know = Magical Transformation. It may have worked too—had Jen not gone and added that unnecessary "u" to her new first name. (If I didn't already know the reference I would have no clue how to pronounce "Satchuel." Way to go with the Black-name stereotype, Satch! Like, you can't be a Nubian gal named Jennifer? Drop one of the "n's" if it will make you feel more authentic.)

Before Satch was outed, there was CV Vitolo-Haddad (pronoun "they"), graduate student at the University of Wisconsin-Madison, who resigned from both their teaching position and their leadership role at the Teaching Assistants Association (TAA), after they confessed that their roots were not Black but Southern Italian/Sicilian. (There was a time in the US when being Sicilian might have been enough for Haddad to pass as Black.)

And, of course, only days before CV came out, the woman who kicked off this hat trick of ethnic fraud was none other than George Washington University's Africana Studies professor Jessica Krug who, according to her confession on Medium, had "eschewed" her "lived experience as a white Jewish child in suburban Kansas City under various assumed identities within a Blackness" that she "had no right to claim: first North African Blackness, then US rooted Blackness, then Caribbean rooted Bronx Blackness."

If you doubt this once self-described "unrepentant and unreformed child of the hood," you can bear witness to Krug at her peak Caribbean-rooted Bronx Blackness in a YouTube clip where her alter ego "Jess La Bombalera" calls in to a New York City Council hearing on police violence.

Let's just say the most authentic thing about La Bombalera's performance is the fact that she, a white woman who moved to New York City from the suburbs of Kansas City, takes a moment to complain about gentrification. Nobody's casting this gringa to voice a Borinquen cartoon character! (Hank Azaria would nail the role though!)

As if foreshadowing her own character's assassination, Krug even calls out, "To all the white people after me, yield your time to Black and brown people."

Now you could get bogged down in the painful comedy of watching Krug attempt to speak like she's from El Barrio or try to dance salsa. (The footage of her dance attempts is no longer available at the link on Twitter where I first found it. And I am happy about that. Although I would love to watch Krug code-switch and turn on her Caribbean-rooted Bronx Blackness to order a *pernil* at my family's butcher shop on 110th, between Park and Lex.)

Sure, her performance is a failure, as are the others'. But how much of race in general is performative? In a world where threats are made to revoke figurative Black cards from actual Black people, what's more important: your phenotype or the script you read out loud in public?

It's rather telling that all these female frauds worked in academia and/or activism—two industries where race, identity, and "lived experience" are major currencies. As Melissa Chen points out, "When there are incentives in the market of identity, you'll have identity entrepreneurs."

I agree with that, but in these particular cases I see more motivation beyond just market incentives.

For example, the editorial director for Duke University Press, poses the following question, now that Krug's been found out, "What are we then to do with her scholarship, which, as it happens, has been widely praised and recognized as important?" (Just think of all the undergraduate and graduate students who are taking on massive debt to study her shit!)

In the case of Satch, she seems to have done some positive things for her community, like founding the No Questions Asked Food Pantry—something critics have pointed out she could have done without masquerading as a Black woman. Sure. But then she would have run the risk of being labeled a "white savior." As we all know: 'Tis better to have never saved than to have saved while being white.

Let's not forget that Rachel Dolezal was married to a Black man and even claimed that she and her family were the targets of several hate incidents.

Now that Dolezal's single, I imagine she's dating other Black men and since she came out as bisexual, she's probably tossing some Black women into the mix. Is there a more sincere way to show you truly care about a cause than by sleeping with your cause?

Actually, I wonder if what we're seeing here are examples of some next-level white saviorship. Like the story of the Christian God who became man, the ultimate white savior is one who becomes Black, shows Black people how to be Black, and ultimately sacrifices her Black identity (when outed).

It's hard to watch all these stories unravel and not think back to Chris Rock's 1999 stand-up special *Bigger & Blacker*, where Rock says, "There ain't a white man in this room who would change places with me. None of you. None of you would change places with me. And I'm rich. That's how good it is to be white."

Twenty-three years later, I can't be certain that a white man would change places with Chris Rock...but a white woman just might. I guess that's progress.

14

ANOTHER WHITE MAN

When Elliot Page came out as transgender, the public praised him. His announcement tweet was liked 1.8 million times, he was congratulated by Hillary Clinton, and Sir Ian McKellen said he was "so happy" for Elliot.

But all I could think was, "Great. Just what the world needs—another white man."

I wanted to reach out to Elliot, grab him by his narrow shoulders and shake him. "Look around, man! Now is not the time to be a white dude!"

Do you really want to be held responsible for every bad thing that has ever happened—and will happen? We're not just talking about oppressing minorities, storming the Capitol Building, and improv comedy. We're talking about even hate crimes committed by *other* races!

As Bishop Talbert Swan of Spring of Hope Church and the Greater Springfield NAACP explained so eloquently on Instagram:

> Anti-Asian racism has the same source as anti-Black racism: white supremacy. So even when a Black person attacks an Asian person, the encounter is fueled very specifically by white supremacy. White supremacy does not require a white person to perpetuate it.

The Bishop's post may have since been deleted—but the vibe still lingers, like woke aftertaste.

There are those who say white men have always had it easy (as if conquering the world is "easy"!), but those days are in the past. Decolonization is where it's at now. (Unless, of course, you're not white, in which case colonize away—just call it something different.)

In short: it ain't all fun and games anymore, as any white man will tell you. Sure, you get "white privilege"—but that won't prepare you for opioid addiction, dying younger than white women, and spending way too much time on Reddit. Probably getting radicalized.

The fact of the matter is the world has too many Elliots and not enough Ellens. And Elliot had to go fuck up the ratio even more!

Yes, I know Elliot is brave for finally embracing his authentic self, but if I could live out the rest of my days as a cute Canadian actress/activist, I would. Sure, I'd be living a lie—but I'd be a living a *little white lie*. Like telling people I saw *Juno*—and loved it![35]

When Elliot came out, I thought, the lil' dude's just gonna make trouble for himself—and influence other white men to come out of the closet. What for? To form a militia?

Watch, I said, Elliot Page is about to start getting paid more money for the exact same roles Ellen Page was playing.

---

35 I still haven't seen *Juno*. Shh…

Although this time around it will take more talent, because he'll be a guy playing girl roles.

Now I'd watch that version of *Juno*![36]

Of course, there are cynics out there who think Elliot made the transition to manhood in order to gain exposure and to kick his career up a notch.

I disagree with those people wholeheartedly. Let's face it—getting a little boy's haircut and donning a baseball cap are one thing, but Elliot went all the way and had a double mastectomy. Top surgery is a pretty radical move to pad your acting résumé!

Not to mention, coming out as a white man today is a terrible career move. As if Hollywood is actively trying to uplift the voices of white men!

If there's any cynicism to be had it has to do with Elliot's insistence that he's nonbinary. His Nonbinary Wiki refers to him as "a nonbinary trans guy." Which I find very confusing.

I can tell you from personal experience that with more mouths to feed in the Perez household I was ready to "come out"—if it meant more job prospects. But whatever identity I chose, I didn't want to have to put in too much work. That's why I was thinking "nonbinary" would be the way to go. Because as the Human Rights Campaign (HRC) website explains it, "Non-binary people may identify as being both a man and a woman, somewhere in between or as falling completely outside of these categories." Which sounds easy enough.

And according to the site's "Transgender and Non-Binary People 101" section, you can even change your gender and not have a gender at the same time!

---

36   No, I wouldn't. But I'd pretend like I did. Shh…

That doesn't make any sense—but, as a comedian, I'm open to not making sense. Call *me* cynical. But don't call Elliot cynical.

No, in fact I think Elliot shows the lengths people will go—both surgically and linguistically—to make sure they are never just another white dude taking up space on the planet.

Hell, the only reason I submitted my DNA to 23andMe was to find out how *not-white* I am and to give my sons a *not-white*, guilt-free chance at life. I know I'm not alone. (If "Latinx" ever takes off I will reevaluate my position on that label too.)

We all know the best thing Malcolm Little did for his career was come out as non-binary.

Excuse me.

The best thing Malcolm Little did for *their* career was come out as nonbinary.

But what worked for Malcom X and other celebrities may not work for Elliot. That remains to be seen. But no matter what, I will be watching.[37]

To be fair: Elliot's transformation wasn't all problematic—it was also inspiring. The most inspiring thing about it was that he turned a lesbian straight. Remember his wife, Emma Portner, married him when they were both lesbians.

For that accomplishment, homeboy Elliot was a hero to men and a god to dudes under 5'2". And the fact that he did it all *without a dick*—woah!

But the dream was short-lived. In January of 2021 Elliot filed for divorce. His former partner, Emma, once said, "Trans, queer and non-binary people are a gift to this world."

Sure. But you know who's not a gift to this world? White men.

---

37   No, I won't. Shh...

And at the end of the day, who the fuck wants to be married to a white man?

Not me.

15

HATE-CRIME WRITERS

Jussie Smollett's hate-crime hoax revealed a few things about the state of our nation:

1) It was evidence that we went one day in the United States without a gay Black man being beaten up by white Trump-supporting racists. And that's something we should all be happy about—especially Jussie Smollett.[38]

2) A wealthy actor had to stage his own hate crime. Think about that. That's how good race relations have become.

3) Hate-crime hoaxes are the one genre of fiction that would certainly benefit from more white male writers.

---

38 Jussie may have been found guilty—but for the first time ever America was innocent.

In *Hate Crime Hoax: How the Left is Selling a Fake Race War*, author Wilfred Reilly documents so many fake hate-crimes that could have used a white man's touch.

Television, film, and the rest of the arts are casting out white men—showbiz is no longer interested in the male Caucasian lived experience—which means there is a large pool of professional white men to draw from for your project. That's not to say you should hire just any white man to craft your hoax. You need to find yourself the right writers—the right *whiters*, if you will.

White allies to the BIPOC and LGBTQ+ causes need not apply. The woke are not going to tell you how they would hate-crime you—unless you're a conservative, maybe. But if that's the case, your victimhood story wouldn't be compelling enough in the first place.

No, you need honest white folks in the room. If you can't staff full-time writers, at least put together a focus group to go over the details of your deception. The last thing you want is for your bullshit story to be blasted out by the mainstream press, only to unravel in the court of public opinion (or worse, as was the case with Jussie, the literal court of the justice system).

Some of these hoaxes are so shitty they wouldn't even need a white racist to make them better.

I remember one hoax in particular from back in 2015. A black graduate student at the University of Missouri went on a "one-man hunger strike," demanding the resignation of the college president, "after a swastika drawn in human feces appeared on a college dorm's brand-new white wall." This was the last racist straw for the student, who claimed it was just one of many racist incidents that had gone down at Mizzou.

Now, if I came across a swastika made of shit, I'd probably not want to eat either. *Shit*—the shit wouldn't even have to be in the shape of a swastika to make me lose my appetite. Call it a "hunger strike," if you like.

But what a weird thing to do, huh? A *poop swastika*.

When I first heard about it, I thought, "Is there any chance drawing a swastika with shit means you *don't* like Nazis?"

I mean, the swastika is a sacred symbol to this specific brand of shitty people.[39] And I have seen swastikas tattooed onto the shitty bodies of Neo-Nazis—the kinds of bodies I imagine Adolf Hitler did not have in mind when he was talking about the Master Race. But even on these gross white supremacists, their swastikas were drawn with care and precision. The tattoo artist didn't just shit it out onto their pasty skin.

With the United States being, for many critics of our country, The Diet Third Reich, you're telling me a person willing to smear shit on a wall—a Phantom Shitter—couldn't find out if such an act would be the best use of their hate-crime hoaxing time?

Reilly covers this incident in his book. According to his research, there may be no definitive evidence that the poop swastika even existed as we were told to believe.

I guess that gives you the opportunity to draw your own poop swastika in your mind and even add a smell to it, if you so desire.

What does a hate-based diet smell like? I wonder—then quickly stop wondering. Because it's making me sick.

---

39   When I traveled to Nepal, I saw swastikas all over the place—it is also a sacred symbol for Hindus. Granted, the Hindu swastika is not tilted the way the Nazi version of it is. In either case, I would never expect to see a devout Hindu or devout Nazi craft one out of a turd.

Ultimately, with hate-crime hoaxes it all comes down to
the writing. So, the next time you're thinking about perpe-
trating a big public fake-out, don't do the false narrative
you're pushing a disservice. Go ahead and hire the *white*
professional.

16

COMEDY'S HR DEPARTMENT

I wish I could quit social media. Not just a few of the platforms—but the whole thing. The longest I have ever gone without it were the two weeks my wife and I were on our honeymoon in France and Iceland, two countries where it is easy to log off, eat, drink, and try to make a baby.

I realized that life is much happier when lived offline—especially when you don't feel the need to post the best takes of your happiness for others to see. (Just scroll down my wall for evidence to back up my claim.)

Overall, social media has been great for me though. Chances are if you're reading this it's because some coder in Silicon Valley is our nexus. Thanks to those smart men on the spectrum, I have been able to find and build an audience online.

There are downsides, of course. Anyone who has ever been the victim of a social media mobbing or has been cancelled can tell you that.

You know, I don't think people get fired anymore for being bad at their job. Instead, their employer waits for them to go viral for any of the reasons you do not want to go viral: writing or sharing the wrong tweet or starring in the latest context-free, thirty-second video recorded on a smart phone.

The only thing I like about cancel culture are the career murder/suicides. That's when the person who gets someone canceled opens him or herself up to scrutiny and ends up getting cancelled too. (Sometimes, by the same mob they whipped up.)

For my purposes, I've been thinking a lot about how social media has blurred the line between comedian and civilian—in that it has given non-comedians the opportunity to dip into comedy by tweeting out jokes or sharing memes here and there and then going about their noncomedy lives.

Most of the people I follow online aren't comedians—and yet they have some of the funniest, most original takes. It's an added challenge to comics—but a necessary one—to stay fresh.

If comedy is your job, you have to create original material and find new angles on topics that have been hammered to death by other comedians, late-night hosts, and now, Kevin in accounting.

It's like the Trump challenge to comedians I described earlier in the book—but for everything!

Where this becomes a problem though is now that Kevin in accounting is mixing it up online, it's like comedians are being judged by the same HR rules that govern Kev's workplace.

Comedians always have been the ones who can say what you're not allowed to say in the office. But now you have scolds demanding comics apologize for their work or take down their offending material.

I used to point to *The Office* as an easy example of the real world versus a fictional world. In the real world, Michael Scott would never make it out of season one of the sitcom with his job intact—but Steve Carrell could make it seven seasons playing the problematic manager at Dunder Mifflin.

We understand the difference between the two worlds. The real world is supposed to punish and stop bad behavior, while the fictional world is supposed to acknowledge the bad behavior and squeeze it for every ounce of funny you can get out it.

Then the most meta thing happened: Comedy Central pulled the "Diversity Day" episode of *The Office* from its rotation. In case you haven't seen it—and if you don't have the DVD box set there's a chance one day you never will—Michael Scott, a white man, made the braindead, insensitive, socially retarded decision to perform Chris Rock's legendary N-word-laden routine "Niggas vs. Black People" in the workplace, and in response corporate is forced to send in a diversity lecturer. By today's standards the episode is problematic—but it's still hilarious. Just like Rock's bit (which I will discuss further, later).

The culture is getting silly. Very silly. I know producers who have had to sit through similar lectures as Michael Scott and his Scranton office had to sit through, lest they risk running afoul of workplace harassment laws.

Comedians have had to listen to corporate attorneys explain to them how improper jokes can constitute harassment in the workplace. How intent doesn't matter—only impact. And how providing a safe and healthy work environment—both on set and in the writer's room—means being very careful about what you say to your creative partners. Because while you might be okay with teasing one another, a third-party who happens to witness it could take offense. And nobody wants that.

Fortunately, we have more options today and not all of us have to sit through a diversity seminar to make a product or a living, which is why I'll probably never be able to quit social media. But I will try to live as much life off of it as I can.

17

IN LIVING COLOR

I grew up in a different time for comedy. Looking back it almost feels like revisionist history.

From prekindergarten through fifth grade I attended P.S. 151 in Woodside, Queens—across the street from the Boulevard Gardens (where I lived) and the Woodside Projects (where my schoolmates lived).

One-Fifty-One is where I got my start in acting. In the first grade I played the Troll in *The Three Billy Goats Gruff*. It was an incredible opportunity—one of those roles that really pushes a six-year-old to his limits. Then there was a lull for a few grades. I didn't act. The work just wasn't there—until the fifth grade, when I played George Washington in *The Betsy Ross Story*, on the origin of the first thirteen-star American flag.

In *The Three Billy Goats Gruff* all the billy goats were played by Black kids. I remember the third goat to enter scene was my friend Teon. Spoiler: Teon got to knock my troll ass off the bridge. (I did my own stunts.)

When it came to *Betsy Ross*, all the other figures of the American Revolutionary War were played by either Black or Puerto Rican kids. I remember a few Chinese classmates were background. And Betsy was played by a chubby Black girl whose name I forget. She wore a satin robe that, I figure, was anachronistic and tight cornrows. I remember the lenses of her eyeglasses were thicker than mine.

We and our teacher/director, Mrs. Arcario, were upending casting norms decades before *Hamilton*!

After playing Washington I wouldn't touch the stage again until a non-speaking role in some murder-mystery in high school—which I did just to pad my résumé for college applications.

Flash-forward twenty years and the more I hear about the lack of representation in film and television today the more I wonder, *what happened?*

Because when I was coming up through grammar school all I remember watching—when I wasn't crushing it on P.S. 151's stage—were Black TV shows.

Eddie Murphy ruled movies. I've forgotten the names of family members, but if you want to reenact *The Golden Child* scene by scene with me, I'm ready to go.

Thanks to illegal cable I got to watch Martin Lawrence's raunchy stand-up. (Look up the line, "*Water would glisten all over your body.*") And on network TV his sitcom may have been rated-G, but *Martin* was still hilarious. His fist-fights with old-lady Ms. Jeri are physical comedy gold and, of course, there's Bruh-Man. Bruh-Man is one of the greatest sitcom creations—a dude who is always breaking into Martin's apartment to make himself a sandwich. Thanks to YouTube, right now you can watch a supercut of Bruh-Man's search for meaning and "sammiches." (Do it....)

I even remember when the show *Roc* started to air live-performance episodes. The cast was made up of incredible stage actors. But after that switch the traditional multicam sitcom turned into something serious. With the show focusing on social commentary, it felt like the sitcom's star Charles S. Dutton—who would later play the inspirational groundskeeper in the film *Rudy*—wanted to deliver intense speeches instead of jokes. It bummed young Luis out. That sort of thing still bums me out.

There was also *Living Single* with Queen Latifah...I can't remember a single episode, but I know I watched them all. If I close my eyes and think back to *Living Single* all I see are strong Black women in pastel suits with shoulder pads.

There were other shows, of course, but the most important one for me was *In Living Color*. The Wayans family is sketch-comedy royalty. My friends and I cracked up recounting the skits we saw on the episode the night before and attempted to do our versions of Damon Wayans' handicapped superhero, Handi-man; antisocial, child-hating Homie the Clown; and everything Jim Carrey did on the show.

In Living Color was of such cultural importance for us that one sixth-grade class even performed a "Men on Films" sketch at an assembly for the entire school.

One Black sixth-grader and one Puerto Rican sixth-grader played the characters Blaine Edwards and Antoine Merriweather, respectively—the Black, flaming-gay film critics from "Men on Films." Think *Siskel and Ebert* meets *Paris Is Burning*. When Blaine and Antoine reviewed *Deliverance*, the Black queens described the man-on-man rape scene as you would a romantic encounter.

I'm certain the boys on stage that morning did not perform *that* bit. I don't know if they performed a skit that had already aired or if they wrote their own—but they were committed to their roles.

They sat at the edge of the stage, legs crossed, and put on the thickest gay lisps their young lips could muster. They weren't dressed for Pride—and unfortunately neither of them had a tiny hat taped to his head à la the character Blaine—but everyone in the audience was howling with laughter. Students and teachers.

Man, I was so jealous not to be up on that stage! I knew I could deliver "two snaps and a twist" just as believably!

This moment only sticks out to me all these years later, because this was normal back then and there is no way it would fly today!

After all, you can't cast straight boys to play gay men—or a light-skinned Puerto Rican to play a Black character.

PUNCHING UP IS
PROBLEMATIC

"To be woke," as John McWhorter put it in *The New York Times*, "was to be in on a leftist take on how American society operates, especially in reference to the condition of Black America and the role of systemic racism within it."

According to McWhorter, "Woke" went from being enlightened and cool to "a handy, nonpejorative replacement for 'politically correct'" in the early 2010s.

At the time I'm writing this, woke has become a pejorative—just like political correctness, social justice, and antiracism. That's as far as I'm concerned. Throughout this book I use woke and its nicknames wokeism and wokeness with its cousins antiracist, PC, and SJW—sometimes interchangeably, but always pejoratively.

Like Donald Trump, woke is a gift to comedy. Sometimes the two complement each other. And like The Donald, when it comes to making fun of wokeness there is always the temptation to let "the jokes write themselves."

There are still hacks out there, calling others "snowflakes," "triggered," identifying as Apache helicopters, and drinking from thermoses tagged with "Liberal Tears."

(Look, neither you nor Ben Shapiro has ever consumed liberal tears. In the case of *The Daily Wire*'s founder I am 100 percent certain of it, because Ben's an Orthodox Jew and liberal tears are not kosher.)

Woke critics of my antiwoke material have made a habit of accusing me of "punching down."

"Comedy is supposed to *punch up*," they say.

Well, when you challenge new sacred cows—like race essentialism, infinite genders, Diversity-Inclusion-Equity, and the Grand Unifying Theory of White Supremacy—sometimes you're gonna "punch down."

I guess.

You know, "punching up" sounds an awful lot like "speaking truth to power." Which got me thinking: When did comedy become all about speaking truth to power, instead of just "speaking truth"?

I don't think the insistence over the past five-plus years on speaking-truth-to-power is as noble as it sounds. Rather, speaking truth to power is politically and socially advantageous for the times we are living in.

Because speaking the truth—without the power component—means sometimes having to call out protected classes of people. Protecting some groups from mockery is a way to shield them and their bullshit from criticism. If you've ever been told you're not allowed to say something because of your immutable characteristics, chances are you're onto something.

Bullshit is the heartbeat of wokeism.

At the 2019 Women in the World Summit, comediennes Judy Gold, Carmen Esposito, Wanda Sykes, and Jenny Hagel talked shop on a panel titled "Can a Divided America Take a Joke?"

Hagel, a writer and performer on *Late Night with Seth Meyers*, explained that when it comes to who can and cannot make jokes, "I think there is a phrase that a lot of people use in comedy, which is 'punching up'…You wanna speak truth to power"—*of course*—"and that making fun of someone who has a higher status than you is a very different act than making fun of someone who is below you."

I appreciate Hagel's explication—but damn is it condescending!

I'm sorry—I can't make jokes about you, because you are beneath me.

It's like the comedy version of women not marrying men who make less money than they do. (All the comedy panelists are lesbians, so I imagine any man they marry would have to be really wealthy.)

Even Hagel's boss, Seth Meyers, is subject to these strict comedy rules. Meyers is a straight white man and therefore not allowed to punch down at groups of people who have "less social power than he does"—which means everyone who is not a straight white man.

His show even has a segment called "Jokes Seth Can't Tell," where Meyers reads the setups and his two diverse women writers, Jenny Hagel and Amber Ruffin, read the punch lines.

The irony is Seth could tell these jokes—they're pretty vanilla—but he picked two women who can't *deliver* them.

"If [Seth] wants to make jokes at lesbians' expense," Hagel tells the panel's moderator, "it kinda feels like a bummer, because he's punching down. That's a group of people who has less social power than he does."

Her point gave me pause. Because I immediately thought about the most successful lesbian on television: Ellen Degeneres. I daresay Seth Meyers—as straight and white and man as he is—would be punching *up* at Ellen.

She's a comedy legend. Worth what? Half a billion dollars. And let's face it: Every morning Ellen stepped out onto that stage to host *The Ellen DeGeneres Show* she knew she could have any mom she wanted in her studio audience.

That. Is. Power.

But who's to say Seth couldn't deliver a joke about eating pussy better than Ellen? With these identity-based restrictions on comedy, we may never know.

To be honest: I'm not very good at intersectional math. When it comes to punching-up versus punching-down, how much wealth does one need to move on up from the social power of a lesbian to that of a mediocre white guy hosting a late-night show on NBC?

What does Hagel have to do to rise in the social hierarchy?

She's an LGBTQ Hispanic woman—a "triple threat," as the moderator calls her jokingly.

That's cute, but there is some truth to it. Back in the day a "triple threat" had to do with talent: acting, dancing, and singing. Now, when quotas are being filled, there is a lot riding on the nontalent of identity.

I refuse to make these calculations with my comedy. I punch all over the place. Ultimately pushing back against group identity in favor of individualism is anti-woke.

Unfortunately these punching-up/punching-down rules—the bullshit tallying of oppression points—have escaped the bounds of comedy.

I've witnessed it with people in real positions of power. Like whenever I satirized President Obama there were bound to be commenters who insisted I was only criticizing him because I had hate in my heart and racism in my DNA.

To be fair: It didn't help that actual racists went after President Obama and First Lady Michelle. But I also made it a point to mock those racists. After a while though, it became clear that most charges of racism are obvious attempts to deflect legitimate criticism.

This should be obvious: No matter what you say, you are never "punching down" at the president of the United States.

One of the early sketches I produced for We the Internet TV was called "Where Have the Anti-War Protestors Gone?"

Did you notice they were eerily quiet during the Obama years compared to the G.W. years?

So, in mockumentary style, I parody a *Vice*-type reporter who has tracked down the US's antiwar movement. It turns out for the last eight years of the Obama administration they've been hanging out in some dude's backyard in Echo Park, Los Angeles.

Through interviews with the dormant activists, my alter-ego learns that the antiwar movement will rise again—once a Republican is elected president. (One of the activists is in literal hibernation until an R gets into office.)

My reporter is trying to find out why these activists, who care so deeply about peace, have let Obama's warring slide. The response (I scripted) to that question turned out to be prophetic.

"Okay, it's like this," a female activist levels with me, "Bush was white. Obama's brown. If you're brown, it's okay to kill other brown people.... It's like saying the N-word."

More recently I saw identity being used to shield then-vice presidential candidate Kamala Harris from criticism. To think people were only criticizing her record as California attorney general for the same reason President Biden chose her as his running mate: because she was a woman of color!

Oh look: Black, Indian, Female—another triple threat! And more jokes Seth can't tell.

If you can't see how silly this stuff is, imagine if every time you criticized Senator Ted Cruz, an online mob accused you of punching down and anti-Latinx racism.

Of course that would never happen. Punching-up and punching-down are also contingent on political association.

Just look at how Black conservatives like Clarence Thomas, Ben Carson, and Larry Elder, et al. are treated. Maybe it's because I'm from a different generation, but I have never felt comfortable hearing white people call Black people "Uncle Toms."

It's almost like white liberals have been saving up all their checked privilege—"doing the work"—and can't wait to spend it.

"Finally! One Black motherfucker I'm allowed to mock!"

When Larry Elder was running against Gavin Newsom in the California recall of 2021, a white woman wearing a gorilla mask chucked an egg at Elder.

You'd think that would be considered punching-down—but the egg flew over his head, so you know she was punching up.

19

THE CHRIS ROCK CHALLENGE

I have never in my life said the N-word without the best of intentions. That streak continues below.

A while back I was invited to be a guest on a new podcast. The host wanted to bring me on to talk with him and his friends about political comedy. They all leaned left, he said, and thought I would bring a diverse perspective to the conversation. I don't lean left and neither he nor his co-hosts were comedians, so I'd be the token comic in a discussion about comedy.

That's one of the side effects of mixing politics and comedy. It allows people who aren't funny to think they're closer to comedians, because they know a little something about politics. They can even invite one onto their podcast to show him just how much they know.

I asked to see the topics they wanted to discuss, so I could prep. The host sent them my way and what became clear was that the goal of the episode was for the left-leaning comedy aficionados to shit on so-called "conservative comedy."

The host even went so far as to write:

> Political satire is a natural ally of progressive politics. Both seek to expose the hypocrisy of those who have, but don't deserve, power. Both are advocating for increasing justice and reducing inequality.

I thanked him for sending me the topics—and for being so candid about his intentions, even if unknowingly—but ultimately I decided to waste my time elsewhere. Hell, I may even have spent some of that time *making* comedy, instead of just talking about it.

I'm not going to challenge the fact that most comedians lean left—if not in their material, then at least in their personal lives.

I'm not going to expend too much energy pointing out that neither the Left nor the Right has a monopoly on hypocrisy. Just pop on *South Park* and watch what comedy gods Matt Stone and Trey Parker do with our endless wellspring of hypocrites.

When it comes to power, I don't feel like unpacking the notion of "deserve." Who deserves power over others anyway? And if those who "deserve it" get it, what does "increasing justice" look like then? Because we can all agree that the "social justice" brand of justice is just a euphemism for revenge.

I'm sure some people would be interested in hearing progressive solutions to inequality—which involve putting control of the economy into the hands of people who can't figure out how to pay back their student loans. Imagine what the national redistribution of humor would look like!

Maybe listeners would dig a history lesson on how progressives today differ from Wilsonian progressives—you know, for the chuckles?

No thanks. Sounds like a lot of work for no money.

Instead, I'd rather listen to progressive lovers of comedy defend the following position:

There's Black people and there's niggas.

And if you're a white progressive—like the aforementioned podcast host—I *really* want to hear your thoughts on this one!

I call it The Chris Rock Challenge.

Anytime I hear someone talking about "truth in comedy," punching up vs. punching down, or "political satire is a natural ally of progressive politics," I'm gonna break it out.

The line, of course, is from Chris Rock's legendary stand-up bit, "Niggas vs. Black People," which you can find in his HBO comedy special *Bring the Pain*.

(Go do that now. The next paragraph will be waiting for you.)

Rock's routine manages to take on politics and culture as it relates to Blacks in the United States. It is edgy, divisive, and hilarious.

You can tell it's hilarious because the audience is losing its shit. Like clapter there is applause—but unlike clapter the applause is drowned out by actual laughter.

I don't think I can reprint the entire transcript below. Not only out of fear of running afoul of copyright issues, but because the words alone won't do Rock's performance justice. (And if I end up doing an audio version of this book, who the fuck am I gonna get to read all these "niggas" out loud?)

Anyway, to kick off The Chris Rock Challenge discuss the following:

> What is the "truth in comedy" of the following statement?
>
> "Every time Black people wanna have a good time, ignorant-ass niggas fuck it up."
>
> Is this line an example of punching up or punching down? Quote:
>
> "Niggas love to *not* know."
>
> And finally, how progressive is this one?
>
> "Shit, a Black man that got two jobs, going to work every day, hates a nigga on welfare."

The whole piece is worth a deep intellectual podcast dive—what I quote above is a good starting point.

Bring the Pain dropped in 1996. There's even a Bone Thugs-n-Harmony reference in it! I was fourteen years old back then. I feel like a fossil now. But I am so fortunate to have grown up watching comedians like Chris Rock, George Carlin, Eddie Murphy, and Martin Lawrence. Comics whose material offers its own challenges to this moment in the 21st century.

In 2000, Rock did an interview with journalist David Bennun that's worth reading in full. It's available on Bennun's website.

> "My viewpoint is the majority viewpoint,
> [Rock says,] that's the crazy thing. It really is.

> There's more people like me than like Tupac Shakur. It's the way most black people think. I wasn't a freak on my block."

So why has it taken so long for somebody to say these things?

> "Because it's threatening to white people, ultimately, that we're alike. Tupac, Biggie Smalls, whatever, that's really not threatening. You can figure that out. And that's always going to be over there. This is the real threat, sitting down in the Royalton and being able to afford anything on the menu. And I don't enjoy being a threat to anybody, I don't get any thrill from that."

I agree that Rock's viewpoint was the majority viewpoint in the 1990s. What I disagree with is the supposed threat that viewpoint poses to white people.

One of the major knocks against respectability politics and assimilation—e.g., the values upon which "Niggas vs. Black People" is built—is that they actually make white people feel comfortable with Black people. So much so that Rock has even been accused of "cooning" and giving ammunition to racists.

But no matter. The comedy piece stands on its own. Back in 2008 president-to-be Barack Obama referenced it on the campaign trail:

> "Too many of our men, they're proud, they brag about doing things they're supposed to do. They say 'Well, I—I'm not in jail.' Well, you're not supposed to be in jail!"

I was twenty-six years old back then, soon to be an Obama voter, and personal responsibility was not only a majority viewpoint—it was common sense. Now common sense is taboo—unless it's something like "common-sense gun control," of course.

By today's standards Rock is delivering a conservative sermon cloaked in a stand-up routine. The kind of messaging you'd expect to hear from a Thomas Sowell, Jason Riley, or Glenn Loury.

Twenty-five years after *Bring the Pain* premiered, Rock was a guest on *The Breakfast Club* morning show, promoting his horror flick *Spiral*. The man doesn't age, but he has matured.

When asked his thoughts on cancel culture and comedy, Rock said:

> When the audience doesn't laugh we get the message...I don't understand why people feel the need to go beyond that... Not letting comedians work is, you know... What happens is everybody gets safe and when everybody gets safe and nobody tries anything things get boring. So I see a lot of unfunny comedians. I see a lot of unfunny TV shows. I see unfunny awards shows. I see unfunny movies. Because everybody's scared to make a move.

Making a move means risking failure—which Rock has made a career out of. He even risked putting out the kind of material that could one day get you called a conservative.

Later in the *Breakfast Club* interview, Rock hedges a little:

If cancel culture helps out people that are marginalized, that's good. If you feel that the fact that people are nervous offending marginalized people is a good thing. Okay. But anything that stops artists from trying, from reaching, that's not good.

I don't speak for all comedians, of course. But if I could come up with a bit on par with "Niggas vs. Black People," I think it'd be worth trying, reaching, and even risking offense for. Give the audience something to laugh about, I say, and the podcasters something to talk about.

20

LAUGH SO HARD IT HURTS

Do you remember the hardest you've ever laughed?
I was probably thirteen years old and my friends Anthony and Mark and I got Chinese takeout from a place on Northern Boulevard. Anthony would always get boneless spare ribs and this time around I got a pint of pork fried rice. I don't remember what Mark ordered. I was too busy shoveling the grub into my mouth as we walked around our neighborhood in Little Neck, Queens.

We're goofing around like we always do and at one point my boys got me laughing so hard that I start choking on this mouthful of pork fried rice. Between laughs I manage to spit some of it out onto the sidewalk, but there are still all these bits of rice and pork and onion lodged inside my throat. I'm losing air. My diaphragm is bugging out.

To the soundtrack of adolescent boys laughing, I cough and cough, trying to will those bits of feed out of my body. Because my anatomy just isn't up to it.

Finally, I can breathe again through my mouth!

But now I notice that my nose is stuffed, and there's a slight burning inside of it.

I have no napkins on me—Mark and Anthony are no help; Ant's still stuffing his face with rib meat—but I do have a T-shirt. I'm wearing it. It's soft and black. So I lift it up, exposing my belly, and then I blow my nose into my shirt. One nostril. Then the other. And again, trying to empty my schnoz....

Gross.

I look at my T-shirt—it's painted with globs of pork-fried-riced snot, like a mixed media collage. I see onion in there too, looking like slivers of plastic—which explains why the burning in my nose is dissipating.

Hilarious.

My friends are bowled over laughing. I can still hear them all these years later. And then I'm laughing again—both in the scene and now.

This time the pain is in my young stomach. I'm taking breaths when my body will allow me.

I want *this pain* to stop too—but not the laughter. But there is no way to laugh this hard without it hurting.

I can't tell you how many times I've laughed so hard it hurts. But it has been a while since the last time. And what feels like a lifetime since that day with the rice.

21

BETWEEN THE 23ANDME

I am upset over the lack of diversity in Hollywood, both on-screen and behind the camera. Of course, when I speak of diversity I am talking about the lack of *me* on-screen and behind the camera.

Until I see myself represented—and I'm not talking about someone who looks like me, I'm talking about *me*, Lou Perez—I won't be happy.

I am the change I want to see. Until I am everywhere, I am nowhere.

Now I may not be able to get there on talent alone and definitely not looks or sexual acumen (I've aged out), but that doesn't mean I'm giving up. I believe the key to future mainstream success may be buried somewhere in my DNA. Thanks to 23andMe, the popular direct-to-consumer genetic testing kit (and the discount it was offering at the time I ordered it), I was able to dig out some of that treasure from my cells.

Feel free to share the following results with any casting directors, managers, studio executives, influencers—anyone who can help me reach the next level in my career's evolution.

Consider this my open call.

CONQUER(OR/ED)

Due to mounting pressure from social-justice activists, a number of professional sports teams made the decision to drop their offensive team names. The Cleveland Indians changed theirs to the Cleveland Guardians. And the Washington Redskins became the Washington Commanders. For a minute they were the Washington Football Team. As literal and awkward as "Football Team" was, it was still far better than Redskins. Other teams whose names are associated with Native Americans should follow Cleveland's and Washington's lead and change theirs as well.

Although I am not a progressive, I agree with them wholeheartedly on this subject of controversy: it is offensive to name sports teams after Native Americans. Because teams should only be named after winners.

Yes, I am allowed to say this, because I am 4.8 percent Indigenous American. (As per 23andMe.)

You are allowed to say this, because it's true. And truth is universal, independent of whose mouth is speaking it.

Plus, you don't have to have any indigenous ancestry or be a historian to know that when it comes to Native Americans, over the years they've got a lot of Ls. Way more Ls than Ws.

Just look at what we're taught in school. Sure, the stuff with the Pilgrims is cute, but after the turkey and stuffing, all we hear about is the genocide, rape, and alcoholism of Native Americans.

Whenever I would catch a Redskins game my mind would inevitably wander to that scene in the film adaptation of Ken Kesey's *One Flew Over the Cuckoo's Nest*, where Chief tells McMurphy about the toll drinking took on Chief's father: "The last time I seen my father, he was blind and diseased from drinking. And every time he put the bottle to his mouth, he didn't suck out of it, it sucked out of him—until he shrunk so wrinkled and yellow even the dogs didn't know him."

…*Touch. Down.*

C'mon—in sports you want a team name that screams, "Victory!" Not perdition and ethnic cleansing!

I guess if there is one group of people who've been oppressed for centuries but still manage to come back and win, it's the Jews. Although I'm not sure a team name like the "Cleveland Jews" would go over so well.

"Hey, did you see the Dodgers destroy the Jews last night?" just doesn't feel right.

(Unfortunately, 23andMe could not detect any Ashkenazi Jewish ancestry for my DNA—0.0 percent—but I am holding out hope for some Sephardic ancestry in my bloodline, for obvious showbiz reasons.)

I can't believe a team hasn't been named after the conquistadors. Well, not since the American Basketball Association's San Diego Conquistadors anyway—but that was back in the 1970s.

Since then we seem to have forgotten just how many wins the Spanish had in the New World before the English took over the league. But to name a team today after the conquistadors would still bring up images of genocide for those in the know. Of course, the conquistadors were on the winning side of that genocide—even with the whole hiccup of bringing syphilis back to the Old World from the New.

But nowadays I don't think anyone would care. Spanish is more associated with Spain's former colonies than with the homeland itself. That's why when an actor like Antonio Banderas wins an award, the world needs to be reminded that he's not Hispanic—he's from Spain—so his victory is another win for the European colonizers and should not be applauded. Or something like that. (If woke Latinos and Hispanics really want to fight back against their colonizers they should refuse to speak Spanish in the first place.)

A few years back my wife and I were in Austin, Texas, for a Young Americans for Liberty event where I was performing. We had finished a Tex-Mex brunch at the restaurant in our hotel and the waiter came back with the bill and the credit card I had given him.

"Your name is 'Pérez?" he said.

"Yeah," I said. I was already adding the tip to the receipt.

"My name is 'Pérez," he said.

"Cool," I said. "We have a very common last name."

"But," he hesitated, as I signed our last name on the merchant's copy of the receipt. "You don't look like a 'Pérez."

Although he had waited on us for close to an hour, this was the first time I noticed him. He was shaken. It was awkward. My wife and I shared a look. Whatever was happening here was a first for us.

The waiter had a thick Mexican accent. Yes, it's the one you're hearing in your head, the stereotype you'd be accused of racism for parroting—and he really leaned into annunciating "*Pérez*." With his pronunciation of it, it may as well have been a different last name altogether. (My signature looks nothing like letters anyway. I could be signing any name.)

I took a good look at his Pérez face. His eyes were dark. They matched his groomed eyebrows. His skin was a few shades darker than mine—but give me a few afternoons in the Austin sun with the vagrants and my melanin would help me close in on the waiter's complexion.

But the only response I could muster was, "Well, you should see my father."

I don't think that satisfied the waiter. He seemed to be searching for something more—an answer—I couldn't give him.

The exchange sure didn't satisfy me either. Those were the days when I was tipping waitstaff 30 percent on my way to a credit score of 800. I gave *this fucking guy* a 30 percent tip!

But the receipt was signed. The tip added. We were done. He walked away from our table, looking more confused and hurt—with no clue that he would one day become an anecdote in this book.

From time to time I think of that interaction/quiet altercation. Sure, it was unprofessional on his part. I was a customer after all. And while I don't subscribe to that whole "The customer is always right" bullshit, I do believe the guy who makes his living carrying your breakfast burrito over to your table shouldn't interrogate you on your identity.

Now I'm wondering what he did with the DNA I left on my coffee cup. If he had the chance I'm sure he would have 23andMe'd me right then and there. (I admit he is partly responsible for me sending my saliva in for testing.)

Regardless of all that, I could have responded to him in a number of different ways. I could have asked to speak with his manager, whom I'm sure had an equally Spanish surname. Or I could have gone on the defensive and went deeper in my Pérez bona fides—make my case with a slide show depicting my family tree on my father's side. But that wouldn't have been me. That would have been the younger me.

No, instead I wish I had made the awkward situation *more awkward* by being honest with him:

"Actually, *camarero* Pérez, I look like the men who conquered your people and gave you my last name."

Trust me. I've seen the Spanish portraits up close in El Museo del Prado in Madrid. If you have a second, Google me. I bet you never thought the conquistadors shared my uncanny resemblance to both legendary comedian Andy Kaufman and Canadian Prime Minister Justin Trudeau. (How is that even possible? Kaufman and Trudeau look nothing alike. I know. But they both look just like me. Once you see it, you can't unsee it. You will never decolonize me from your mind.)

I guess there is only so much you can do with the human genome. This is what was done with mine—which is, according to 23andMe, 94.1 percent European, and when broken down further, 34.6 percent Spanish and Portuguese.

Combine that with my indigenous heritage—and the repercussions of conquest are evident in my very DNA, man! My double helix is stolen land! #Colonizer! #Colonized!

I might not be that far removed genetically from the waiter who shares my last name. I should have asked for some of his spit to send in for testing. Maybe we could team up and pool our genetics—at least the variants left over by history's victims.

I wonder how much I could lean into this new information about my identity. Is it too late for a forty-year-old man like me to change overnight—to update my CV? Is 4.8 percent of anything enough to get away with that?

Can I feign outrage over hot white coeds wearing head-dresses to outdoor EDM events? Can I get upset over the production of fake dream catchers when neither the fake nor the real ones actually catch dreams? I'm not looking to take an ayahuasca trip anytime soon—can I be bothered that some tech bros decide to make a long weekend out of puking themselves to a higher level of consciousness? Or any of the other examples of pan-Indigenous cultural appropriation?

Even though I have the genes to back it up, I still feel like I'd be faking it, not unlike the white girls I talked about earlier who went all *Dolezal*.

Can I still cash in on victimhood without actually being a victim or even feeling like one? Am I a good enough performer to get away with it?

PEOPLE OF COLOR

I was at an open mic one night and the comedian who went up before me was Indian American—not Native American (like yours truly). I had seen him before with his beautiful black hair hanging below his shoulders—but tonight he had it up in a man bun. He had a vibe about him—I'm thinking Bay Area. The kind of guy you'd see interviewed in *The Problem with Apu*.

He was trying out this bit about an encounter he had with a cop and—well, the way I explain it is that sometimes a comedian will share an anecdote from his life, but in the telling of it you realize, "No. This never happened. You're trying to make this bit autobiographical—but it's not working." This was one such bit.

"Yeah, man," he said, as if to motivate himself not to give up on the fantasy just yet. "You know how cops talk to *us*—*People of Color*. You know what I'm saying!"

And he points to a Black comic sitting in the front row of the audience. That comic did his set earlier in the night, but was kind enough to stick around to support the rest of us. It's rare to see a comic do that. But there was no sign of shared experience on his face. He hadn't even brought up law enforcement in his set—and he had six minutes in which to do it, if he had wanted to.

When I got to the microphone, I was inspired. I asked the same Black comic in the front row if he ever gets upset over this "People of Color" stuff.

He didn't seem to enjoy being a target of crowd work two comics in a row. He shook his head, "No." So I decided to be upset for him—which is a thing called "Giving voice to the voiceless."

"Well, it pisses me off!" I said. No one in the room knew where I was going with this. Neither did I really. But I committed to it and called out the previous comic of color. "You know, I'm more likely to be shot by a cop than you are. Statistically speaking. So, why don't you sit this one out? Don't try to get in on the struggle."

I had seen it a number of times before. One day I overheard a lady describe herself as a "woman of color." I turned to look and almost corrected her. "Woman of color? *Girl*, you're Korean."

What has her nonwhite, Korean existence been like in the United States? I wondered. *What was her struggle? Choosing which Jewish guy to marry?*

In what neighborhoods did these people live where *they* were people of color?

Having grown up in Queens and with my biography—I'm talking even before I got my DNA tested—this labeling is so alien to me. I know that back in the day people would try to pass as white. But today, we see the reverse and the lengths to which people will go to pass as anything but white. The whole POC thing seems so fraudulent: the invention of a white vs. nonwhite binary. As if all white people are the same and all nonwhite people get along.

When I used to spend more time at my family's butcher shop, it was not uncommon to hear our African-American clientele tell our Mexican employees and Senegalese customers to "Go back to your country!" respectively. (Although I bet they didn't give a shit which country the immigrants went back to, as long as they got the fuck out of East Harlem.)

I don't know if we've reached peak POC yet—or maybe it's more like the nadir—but the "Race Card Project" that ran in *National Geographic* is pretty damn close to it.

The project bills itself as, "Our honest, hidden thoughts on race captured in just six words." But what it manages to do is to capture some of the most boring people imaginable—the kinds of people you don't remember from high school—and the only thing they have going for them is their relationship to and from whiteness.

It is a sad time capsule that nails our race-obsessed culture. One of the submissions reads "Native Americans, America's invisible invisible invisible." Imagine being so held-down that even editing your six-word submission would be deemed an act of oppression.

The project features a white woman who states "I'm ashamed for my ancestors' race." As expected. Now imagine being this person. This is your time to shine—your opportunity to live on forever in a publication like *National Geographic*—and you choose shame?

My favorite six words in the collection are: "Black Boy. White world. Perpetually exhausted." It's penned by a chubby Ethiopian whose family fled the perpetual strife of their homeland in exchange for perpetual exhaustion and carbs in the United States.

I have a theory about the label People of Color. It seems like an attempt to appropriate Black pain—a unique historical pain in the United States—without actually having to be Black. Because if I'm in pain, if I'm a victim—that is, if I too am declaratively nonwhite—then there's no way I could be victimizing you, Black person. I am innocent.

You may disagree with me on this, but my 0.8 percent North African DNA is saying, "Preach, Brother Lou!"

The fact that the taxonomical term "BIPOC" had to be created tells me that I'm on to something. Look, when grievance is a commodity—and a finite resource at that—you can't just let it be redistributed evenly to every nonwhite person around. There are levels.

So, POC's have to take a step back and bow to the more-persecuted and less-privileged Blacks and Indigenous peoples of the POC coalition.

But even within the made-up BIPOC community there are tensions. On an episode of PBS's *African American Lives* with host Henry Louis Gates Jr., actor Don Cheadle finds out that he is the descendent of Black slaves, but that his ancestors were not owned by white slaveholders but rather by Native Americans. Cheadle's ancestors were owned by members of the Chickasaw Nation, who, as a sovereign nation, continued to keep slaves even after the end of the American Civil War. His ancestors are eventually emancipated. The story is so fascinating.

I went down this rabbit hole only after reading *The 1619 Project*'s Nikole Hannah-Jones broach the subject of Indian slaveowners in a Twitter spat with whom I believe was another BIPOC. (They may have just been a POC. I don't remember. But if I'm wrong, I offer my sincerest apologies to the individual of color I may have offended.)

You know, in a world where identity is currency and history is fucking wild, man, you're going to eventually need to make a term like "ADOS"—American Descendants of Slaves—to separate yourself from the others. You may be Black, but are you "slave" Black?

Unfortunately, I am neither. If only—oh the places my career would go!

NEANDERTHAL

As much fun as it was to peek into my DNA, I can't bring myself to hang too much of my identity on this stuff—even if it means career stagnation.

Do you want a good laugh?[40]

According to 23andMe:

> We did not find evidence of your ancestry in the following locations.
>
> Confidence level for Argentina: Not Detected

There is 0.0 percent Argentinean in my DNA!

This news would have been soul-crushing for young Luis to hear. The young man's personae was so dependent upon his father and his homeland: San Miguel de Tucumán, *El Gaucho Martín Fierro*, and the butchering of beef.

---

40 Finally!

I find it hilarious though! A more desperate man would call up his dad—"Dude, what the fuck?"—and seek to pivot into some other identity marker.

Now, say I chose to go that way—down the road of desperation—what else do you have for me, DNA?

"All together, Lou," 23andMe says, "your Neanderthal ancestry accounts for less than 2 percent of your DNA."

"I'm listening...."

"You have more Neanderthal DNA..." Drum roll. "...Than 56 percent of other customers."

"Hell yeah!"

Talk about oppressed!

"People of Color"?

Shit, my Neanderthals died out 40,000 years ago! The only remembrance my archaic ancestors get are in the 243 variants found in my DNA!

Why am I yelling, as I type this?

Because I'm part Neanderthal, you Homo sapien motherfuckers! This is how we do!

You can't imagine how hard we've had it! Try looking like a Neanderthal and getting a human chick to sleep with you—30,000 years before alcohol was even invented!

I got it rough, man! My people are struggling out in these *sapien* streets! No one is naming a sports team after us extinct freak losers!

I may be a proud descendant of Neanderthals, but I am still cursed. I am still a victim. I have two variants associated with having a worse sense of direction, one variant associated with a fear of public speaking, four variants associated with being a better sprinter than distance runner, one variant associated with being less likely to prefer salty foods over sweet, and one variant associated with having more dandruff!

Where. The. Fuck. Is. My. Sitcom?

(I promise to write in a Black character. They can be my ADOS best friend.)

STUPID REPRESENTATION

When you see a stupid character on-screen, do you feel represented?

If your answer is no, you may be too stupid to recognize yourself. And chances are you love the movie *Idiocracy*.

Although it came out in 2006, I had never seen the Mike Judge cult classic until about a year ago. And the reason I finally watched it was because during the Trump years I kept seeing commentary and memes online with some version of "We are living through *Idiocracy* right now."

In the movie the good-looking Wilson brother, Luke, plays an average guy who's put in suspended animation along with a prostitute played by Maya Rudolph. They wake up 500 years in the future to see what happens when smart people stop breeding and only the dumdums are rutting. The movie is basically a proeugenics sketch comedy stretched out to an unnecessary hour and twenty minutes.

Even though it came out over fifteen years ago the cast of dumb fucks in *Idiocracy* is pretty diverse. The people who should be sterilized for the good of humanity—even if that means *the end of humanity*—come in all shades. It's a more inclusive version of early 20th century progressivism.

I love Mike Judge's work—but I don't like this movie. Now if I had seen it in 2006 I would have loved it. Back then twenty-four-year-old Luis thought of himself as far from a dumb fuck as you can get. In fact, as a graduate from NYU, Luis's balls carried the kind of sperm that could stop humanity's spiral into *Idiocracy*.

What a selfish young man he was! Wearing condoms. Pulling out. Not donating his swimmers. The least he could have done is save a few ounces of semen for the greater good. He had so much room in his freezer back then—those were the days of his bachelorhood when he was eating out or ordering in every night.

But no. Each night Luis did not get a woman pregnant our timeline moved one step closer to watering crops with Brawndo—"Brawndo's got what plants crave. It's got electrolytes."—which, according to anti-MAGA resistance fighters online, gets you Trump in 2016 and Trump 2024 lawn signs sprouting like weeds today.

I don't know that young man Luis anymore. Time and fatherhood have chipped away at my arrogance and my hairline—but not my fertility. My first son was conceived when I was thirty-seven. The second one when I was thirty-nine. It's too soon to tell what impact, if any, my sperm is going to have on the future. But what I do know is that I am not prepared for dystopia.

As I write this, my house is being renovated and I can barely handle that coordinated chaos. The place is now unlivable, but one day it will be livable. Yet I have none of the skills or knowledge to help bring that day closer. I'm useless. (If you sit on your hand until it goes numb, it feels like someone else is signing your checks to contractors.)

Yeah, I'm softer now. I worry more. I find myself saying, "I don't know" a lot. Maybe too much.

When was the last time you heard someone say, "I don't know"? Or seen it typed out in the comments section?

When was the last time *you* admitted, "I don't know"?

It's hard to admit you don't know something when you can just Google it—in a world overpopulated with people who think telling you to "Google it!" is a finishing move. You know, *#Destroyed #Owned.*

The goal of an internet argument isn't to win—it's to waste the other person's time. Googling can be just that. Because whatever "it" is, having access to all the info doesn't guarantee I'll understand it. Like, I used to be really interested in IQ—until I found out what my IQ is.

I know I'm not alone.

That's why I find it funny to see so many people prefacing their statements with things like "Speaking as a woman…" or "Speaking as a person of color…. " Especially when arguing with others.

But I never hear anyone begin a sentence with, "Speaking as a stupid person…."

Even on this chart of "Intersecting Axes of Privilege, Domination, and Oppression" the word "Stupid" is missing. (See next page.)

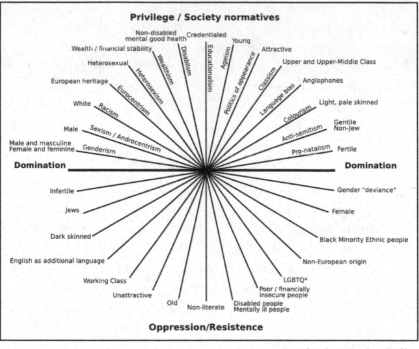

Privilege / Society normatives

Non-disabled
mental good health　Credentialed
Wealth / financial stability　　　Young
Heterosexual　　　Disablism　Attractive
European heritage　Wealthism　Educationalism　Upper and Upper-Middle Class
White　Heterosexism　Ageism　Anglophones
Male　Eurocentrism　Politics of appearance　Light, pale skinned
Male and masculine　Racism　Classism　Gentile
Female and feminine　Sexism / Androcentrism　Language bias　Non-Jew
Genderism　Colourism　Fertile
Anti-semitism
Pro-natalism

Domination ————————————————————— **Domination**

Infertile　　　　　　　　　　　　Gender "deviance"
Jews　　　　　　　　　　　　　Female
Dark skinned　　　　　　　　　Black Minority Ethnic people
English as additional language　　Non-European origin
Working Class　　　　　　　　　LGBTQ*
Unattractive　　　　　　Poor / financially insecure people
Old　Non-literate　Disabled people
Mentally ill people

Oppression/Resistence

Graphic by Natalya Dell

You've got identifiers like "Young" and "Attractive" and "LGBTQ*"—and of course, race and ethnicity—represented. But no Stupid. Which makes me wonder if these axes were put together with…scientific rigor.

Because whether you like it or not, if you're stupid, it's a huge part of your intersectional identity.

Based on what is included, I guess one could argue that "Disabled"/"Mentally ill" or "Non-literate" is potentially stupid? Sure. But really, all these groups are potentially stupid.

What I think happened is they left *Stupid* out of this matrix, because the goal is to quantify privilege. And stupidity is just going to fuck up the calculations. Because stupidity is universal—it transcends and overlaps with race, creed, sex, gender, class. All the categories of human.

Look around you: all these intersectional dumb fucks going about their days! Stupid oppressors and stupid oppressed-ees!

Something else to note: nowhere on these axes is the category "Asshole." Imagine that. Think about all the assholes you've met. Being an asshole is often an asshole's defining characteristic. You may even be an asshole yourself. Have you met yourself lately?

A friend of mine pointed out that the word "Asshole" might be missing from the mockup—but all the lines lead to what looks like a butthole. (See above.) To be fair, my friend is a credentialed, heterosexual, masculine male, fertile, and a Jew of non-European origin—so…I don't know what to do with that information. *The drawing looks like a butthole.*

I get that no one wants to admit to being an asshole. Just like no one wants to admit to being stupid. We live in a time where declaring your group identity lends whatever you're about to say an air of authority.

"This is how I identify—therefore what I'm about to tell you should be respected and taken seriously…*Idiocracy* is prophecy!"

Unlike the other categories you're not going to gain points when your opening salvo is "Speaking as an asshole…" or "Speaking as a stupid person…"

Imagine "Speaking as a stupid asshole…I'm about to say some stupid shit and you better not check me on it. Because if you do, I'm gonna *asshole* all over you!"

Forget it.

As much as I would like to see a future where people openly admit their stupidity, I don't know if it would necessarily be a better world—President Camacho could still win election—but it would definitely be a more honest world.

And on the representation front, if more people admitted they were stupid they would magically see themselves more often on-screen. Forget quotas. Forget debates over colorism and other discriminating factors. There would be a glut of stupid representation. Shit, there would be stupid *overrepresentation*!

We might even start hearing critics say Hollywood is too inclusive! With too many dumb fucks represented!

23

MASKHOLE[41]

If COVID-19 had a PR team, it could not have picked a better time to drop its novel virus than during a Donald Trump presidency. As an American and a New Yorker, I had the wonderful misfortunate of being angry at my president, my governor, my mayor, and my neighbors—who all did their part to make sure this virus went viral.

Back in March–April 2020, I was a new father, spending way too much time online, trying to discern fact from fiction, good-faith arguments from political posturing, and navigating the masks vs. no masks debate. And I was paranoid. Like *really* paranoid.

Sure, I was still able to goof—to say things like, "I want my coronaviruses made in America—not China!"[42]—but

---

41 A version of this chapter was first published in *Spiked* as "The real mask-holes."

42 This was back when the lab-leak theory was being brushed off as a conspiracy theory and even worse, racist! As many others have pointed out, it's weird that the nonracist COVID-19 origin story was that it came about because the Chinese will eat whatever the fuck they can get their mouths on.

still. I was perfect for my neighborhood of Brooklyn Heights, where paranoia and neuroses are included, like water and heat, in your monthly maintenance charges.

I washed my hands countless times a day with soap. And dried them out in between thirty-second paw baths with Purell or whatever hand sanitizer we could get our hands on (and on our hands).

But how could I know for sure if my mitts were really clean? Even the most reliable hand-san was only killing 99.9 percent of germs—and what about the cheap shit that smelled like bathtub margaritas?

Look at your hands right now. Are they clean?

The virus could be anywhere, you know—on any surface! I thought. *And on or in* anyone!

Every time I went to the supermarket I felt like I was embarking on a suicide mission, or worse—a murder/suicide of myself, my wife, and our newborn. I was living out a dystopian nightmare—where food was still abundant (if just a little pricier than usual), my credit cards still worked, streaming services were still streaming, and Amazon was still delivering. But was the risk of opening the cardboard shipping box worth what was inside it?

The stress took its toll on me during what should have been my amazing first months of fatherhood. Fortunately, among the many links to conspiracy theories that friends and family were sending me—not the ones that turned out to be true, mind you—one particular text came through with a link to a YouTube video titled: "Empowering Talk: Protecting Families During COVID-19 Pandemic" by Dr. David Price of the Weill Cornell Medical Center. It is still up on YouTube, so I figure it doesn't run afoul of any corporate/state community guidelines.

Dr. Price's purpose for making the video was to supplant fear of the disease with empowerment. To replace the unknown with the known. I was definitely in need of that. All of that. I'm already very good at catastrophizing—I didn't need any help from a pandemic.

To sum up the video: Wash your hands, don't touch your face, and don't spend too much time unprotected with someone who is infected.

I was relieved to get this information—even more so to hear that this plague wasn't dooming babies. But still I worried about my parents, who, because of their ages and comorbidities, were at a higher risk of serious symptoms from the virus. A month before our son was born—and days before my thirty eighth birthday and a string of shows to promote a documentary I produced about Democratic Socialism and Sweden—my father was admitted to the hospital for what doctors first thought was a stroke, then Bell's palsy, and then finally, the correct diagnosis: Guillain-Barré syndrome.

My wife and I made our bubble a compact one. On the weekends we would see her parents one day and mine the other. No traffic in either direction in those days—which was the best part of the plague. This was well before COVID-19 testing was available.

I remember reading a new mother's lament on social media nearly a year into this thing—when testing was finally available everywhere—that her baby had yet to meet her grandparents.

"It was just too much of a risk," the mother wrote.

A year? I thought. *Really? No, I bet you just don't want to see your parents.*

To be fair, maybe those new grandparents were shitty people. But I think COVID-19 gave a lot of people a reason to skip out on their families and for some to stop living life in general.

In the case of my wife and me, it would have been undeserved punishment to keep our child away from his grandparents. It was a couple months before they met him for the first time and from a distance. We thought we were doing the right thing—the safe thing—but it was cruel to not let them hold him. Not even touch his little feet. Not yet.

And that's what so much of this comes down to. Anyone who wants to live as full and productive a life as possible needs to do his own risk-assessment—if not for his own good, then at least for the good of his children.

That is why it is so important to find out where the science ends and the paranoia begins. I'm afraid too many people just aren't there yet. (Note today's date…. Yep—still not there.)

* * *

Back in July of 2020 I noticed a new COVID-19 fad: Every day, new videos were being posted on social media of "maskholes"—that is, people who refuse to wear masks in public.

The ones I watched were always recorded on smartphones and usually took place in big-box stores in the United States. You don't need that much footage to publicly shame someone nowadays—especially if they're having a meltdown on camera. And in those days of COVID-19, even just a few seconds of bare face would do the trick.

As much as I got a kick out of my fellow Americans who believed it was their constitutional right to enter a private establishment without a face-covering—even if store policy demanded they wear one—I had yet to meet such a patriot in real life. But online was a different story, where depending on the thread I was following, I felt outnumbered because I didn't think businesses that insist I wear a mask when entering their stores were on the same level as Nazis.[43]

I would love to see the Venn diagram of those who believe a baker has the right to refuse to make a cake for a gay wedding and those who believe that same baker has no right to tell customers they are only allowed in his bakery if they are wearing masks.

Twitter aside, I did not have any real-life run-ins with *those* maskholes. After all, I was living in a bougie Brooklyn neighborhood, where even the kids wore surgical masks. So, all the maskholes I have ever encountered have been *wearing* masks.[44]

That's right—you can wear a mask and still be an asshole. (I actually think this version of the slur makes more sense. Because if you're not wearing a mask, shouldn't you be called a "*NO*maskhole"? Or even better: "FaceHole"?)

In July of 2020 I was no longer scared of nor paranoid about COVID-19. I was empowered and embracing life. I wanted to spread some of that around. I wanted to be a good neighbor, you know.

So at 7:00 PM every night I joined in with the rest of my neighborhood and applauded our frontline healthcare workers. I couldn't see any of my neighbors who were also making noise—they were all locked in their apartments—but I could hear them for sure. I never knew for how long we were supposed to applaud the frontliners—or what day

---

43   Then again: I have no idea if Anne Frank was or was not wearing a mask when she was hiding out in that attic—or when the Gestapo captured her.

44   Every maskhole I ever dealt with was wearing a cloth mask to boot. The less-effective your mask is at protecting against COVID-19, the more likely you are to stop and scream at other people for not wearing one.

we all stopped doing it altogether—but I had been a part of that cheer squad.

The other neighborly thing I did was wear a mask when appropriate. I would put one on when entering or leaving the building where I lived.[45] I wore one inside stores and restaurants. (In New York City outdoor dining was back around that time, so once I was seated at a table the mask came off.) And, if I happened to be passing someone on the street, and they were wearing a mask, I'd be courteous and put mine on too.

Mind you, it was the same mask I was putting on and taking off and stuffing into my pocket. Sure, my decision when and when not to don the dirty cloth was not always based in science. But I was trying. Well, more like I *looked like* I was trying.

I spoke with Dr. Amesh A. Adalja, a senior scholar at Johns Hopkins Center for Health Security, for an article I was writing at the time about maskholes for *Spiked Magazine*. Dr. Amesh was another medical expert who helped to put me at ease—this time on the subject of masks. According to him, when we spoke, masks should be worn in situations where you are unable to social distance—that is, if you are going to be within six feet of others, particularly indoors or in crowds, and that close contact is going to last between ten to fifteen minutes.

The virus is not spread through "fleeting contact," as he put it, like going for a walk or a jog—or encountering a maskhole outdoors. And that was something to be thankful for. Having good information really helps to open your world and your place in it. Far too many people in my neighborhood were trapped indoors and trapped within the bounds of their own ignorance and their own fears—

---

45   Eventually masked entrance and egress became co-op policy.

like they had constructed studio apartments within their studio apartments.

There were other things to be thankful for too: like how the virus wasn't particularly harmful to children and how doctors were developing treatments for those who came down with it—not to mention the vaccines that would be developed later.[46]

My wife and I were cramped in our one-bedroom apartment with our newborn—who was developing nicely. That is, he was hitting every sleep regression on time. Now, what's good for baby's health is not necessarily good for his parents'. Sleep-deprived Mommy and Daddy took every opportunity we got to go outdoors. We couldn't sleep, but we could get air. So we did, strolling sans masks to the Brooklyn Heights Promenade, Brooklyn Bridge Park, and down our favorite street, Willow Street.

Masked Brooklynites outdoors always confused me. These were educated people, registered Democrats, professionals who "followed The Science"—and yet I would see them in parks or on otherwise empty streets with their mouths and noses covered. Protecting no one—neither themselves nor others.

Wearing a mask when you're sitting alone in a park is like masturbating while wearing a condom. You look so foolish, you might as well be doing both at the same time. (With the way the city was going I don't think the NYPD would even write you a ticket for it. Maybe give you a "Finish up and get outta here!")

One day I even saw a bicyclist riding while wearing a helmet and a mask—which screamed "safety"—but his eyeglasses were all fogged up. No clue if he made it down the block.

---

46 *Thanks, Donald Trump!* My favorite Trump supporters are the ones who praise Trump for the rollout of COVID-19 vaccines they refuse to take. Owning the libs twice! I guess.

Whatever my neighbors were following to get them to this level of prophylaxis, it sure wasn't The Science. And yet I'd catch their eyes staring at me in judgment. As if I were some heathen openly worshipping a lesser Science.

One night a maskhole who lived in our building attacked another resident for the crime of...not wearing a mask... outside the building, in the street, in the bike lane, while on a bicycle.

That maskhole went on to deputize himself, patrolling our building and neighborhood for other violators. I don't think he has children—but paranoia has given him this baby. (And it's led to more than one police report filed against him.)

On one particular weekend stroll with the family I was pushing our son in his Doona down Clinton Street. With my wife close beside me, we had the sidewalk to ourselves. No one in front of us and no one behind us. The weather was perfect. It felt like we were grabbing B-roll for an indie film.

I began to hear someone a few paces behind us, talking loudly on a phone. As the person got closer, I could make out that it was a woman speaking and what was weird is that the subject matter of her conversation had to do with people not wearing masks...*the zeitgeist!*

As her voice gets louder, it seems like she's drawing closer to us, so my wife and I, we pull the stroller over to the side to allow this person to walk by us. But instead of passing us, the woman crosses the street.

She and I catch eyes. She is Black, middle-aged, and dressed in Spandex workout gear. You know the kind where the leggings and sports bra almost touch, leaving this belt of flesh around the torso?

The mask she's wearing is not Spandex and it's clear that she's pretending to be on her phone.

"Are you talking about us?" I call out to her.

I don't think she was prepared to be asked this question, let alone answer it. I don't know if it's because some folks have been locked in for too long. They don't have loved ones. They don't have real relationships. So the only way they can actually feel human is to initiate any sort of human interaction. Even if it's one of conflict.

But since so many people try to avoid conflict, these shit-starters get used to it being a one-sided thing. You know, the whole attitude of *I can talk shit and no one is gonna do a damn thing about it!*

She hollers back, "Mind your fucking business!"

Ha! I thought. (It may have come out of my mouth too in the moment.) It can be a struggle to remain courteous in an increasingly uncourteous world. And I have to admit: "Mind your fucking business!" is pretty good advice. But her passive-aggressive ass made it my *bidness.*

So I called her an asshole. I called this unidentified M-hole an A-hole.

She got very upset with this. So upset in fact that her first comeback was to call me "Brad." Which I didn't know was an insult.

I did have my COVID hair going—because salons had only just reopened and I hadn't booked an appointment yet—so I guess I looked like I could be a Brad. But then again: A name is a name. I could have been a Muhammad too. Or whatever the fuck her maskhole name was.

As my party of three and her party of one continue to create more distance between each other—I am pushing a four-month-old, remember—she decides that she's going to actually use her phone now. She's not going to pretend to make a call this time—no, she is going to record the rest of this contentious encounter.

It's an all-too-common phenomenon. Even before the world masked up it was a problem. When it comes to narrative, so much depends on the thirty seconds you capture on your phone. Hardly anyone is interested in what led up to those thirty seconds that went viral—what should have been, at worst, "fleeting contact."

I was well aware of that. So I decided not to give in to temptation and continue our back-and-forth—or to even break out my own recording device.

As we walk away, she yells out, "White boy!"

See, "White Boy" is a synonym for "Brad." And she follows up "White Boy" by yelling out, "Your White Wife too!"[47]

I don't know when "white" became a putdown. Years ago I thought whatever white privilege I have there is no fucking way I'm checking it. On the contrary, I married a blonde to get more of it.

I am doubtful this woman would be interested to hear the results of my 23andMe though. It wouldn't change her material in our roast battle.

Were it not for my wife and son, I might have gone back at her by highlighting her FUPA and bad weave, or that she was living proof that women of color are just as capable of being annoying as white women. If you think "Karens" aren't diverse, then you're a racist.[48]

---

47 NB: My white wife is the only wife I have.
48 Instagram decided this insight—both truthful and inclusive—went against their "Community Guidelines on hate speech or symbols." The post was removed from my IG account.

* * *

The mask is a tool that unfortunately became a symbol. What that symbol means depends on the maskhole and what tribe they have aligned themselves with.

In the scene with Black Karen I was either "Brad the Patriot" or "Brad the Murderer." "Brad, Whose Real Name is Luis, and Wears His Mask When It's Reasonable to Do So"? Well, that's just too much work.

I may not have been paranoid about the virus, but I was worried. I was worried about all the things a new father worries about. And I was worried about all the people who think saying "Follow the Science" means they have science on their side and that their attempts to "save lives" through public shaming were worth the costs of making those lives around them miserable.

Trapped around people I did not want to be around, the city was getting to me—changing me. And I was becoming someone I did not want to become.

You can tell a lot about a person by how they react to good news. When I was celebrating the advent of the vaccines, for example, pundits like MSNBC's Rachel Maddow were lamenting the upending of the Masked-vs.-Unmasked Universe:

> I feel like I'm going to have to rewire myself so that when I see somebody out in the world who's not wearing a mask, I don't instantly think, you are a threat or you are selfish, or you are a COVID denier and you definitely haven't been vaccinated. I mean, we're going to have to rewire the way that we look at each other.

Who would have thought that masks would help us really see one another?

24

ALPHA CUCK

Every day I ask myself, "Lou, are you willing to risk offending that person you don't remember from high school?"

And every day my answer is the same: Yes. Yes, I am. I'm even willing to risk offending the people *you* don't remember from high school.

Depending on which video or joke of mine you come across first, you could make all kinds of sweeping assumptions about where I stand on every other subject or policy. It's one of the many downsides of world views devoid of nuance. But the upside is it's a lot of fun fucking with people. Especially ideologues. And I have learned a lot from fucking with ideologues.

When I offend people on the Left, they get the joke—but don't think it's funny. And they think I'm a bad person for making it. They try to #Destroy me with shame.

When I offend people on the Right, they don't get the joke—and don't think it's funny. And they think they can kick my ass. They try to #Destroy me with intimidation.

To the Left, I say, you're not going to shame me. Check out my early work—I got all my shames out years ago. Comedy continues to be a dependable shield.

As for those on the Right talking smack to me, I hope we never meet up in real life…because some of you can definitely kick my ass. If your profile picture has an American flag and a bald eagle in it there's about a 25 percent chance you can fuck me up.

The other 75 percent of online patriots are suspect though. Because one of the worst things Donald Trump did was trick beta males into believing they are alphas. Just because you've watched the UFC doesn't mean you know how to fight. The convergence of MAGA bravado and keyboard warfare was something I dealt with during the Trump years.

I was called "snowflake" and "libtard." But what I miss most is being called a "cuck."

For those of you unfamiliar with MAGA parlance, "cuck" is short for cuckold, which is a man who lets other men have sex with his wife.

First off, that sounds really hot! (If you wanna take five, a simple online search will bring up all sorts of enjoyable examples of cuckoldry.)

Second, my wife and I have only been married four years. We're just not there yet. I'm not ready to share a straw with another man, let alone the mother of my children.[49]

Finally, what makes the cuck insult so hilarious is, as Robert Tracinski pointed out on Twitter:

---

49   Plus, she has terrible taste in men.

> It's ironic that Trump supporters use "cuck"
> as an insult, given that the most famous
> cuckolds in America right now are Roger
> Stone and Jerry Falwell, Jr.

Roger Stone, friend and advisor to Donald Trump, is open and unapologetic about he and his wife being swingers. He talks about the lifestyle in the documentary about him, *Get Me Roger Stone*. In that same doc I also learned that Stone has a tattoo of Richard Nixon in the middle of his back and often dresses like a Batman villain. Whether you like the man or not you can't deny Stone is an interesting cat.

An article in *The Daily Mail* reportedly traced a sex advertisement back to Stone: "Hot insatiable lady and her handsome body builder husband, experienced swingers, seek similar couples or exceptional muscular well-hung single men." (Ooh—that's a lot of assonance!)

Can you imagine being at that orgy?

You're an exceptional muscular well-hung single man—named Luis, perhaps?—and, while you're giving it to Mrs. Stone, you look up to see the naked back of her husband with a sweaty Dick Nixon smiling back at you.

So. Hot.

In the case of Jerry Falwell Jr., Liberty University's former school president, he was apparently into watching other men bang his wife. I'm not going to say that his father, devout Evangelical Christian, Jerry Falwell Senior, didn't have an impact on his son's life, but when it comes to the bedroom it looks like Falwell's smut-peddling rival, Larry Flynt, had a bigger influence.

I guess cuckolding is the kind of kink conservatives can get behind, because ultimately it's promoting marriage.

Whenever a guy would call me a cuck online I would always check out his profile. And every time I did I'd be disappointed. Sure, there was a 25 percent chance he could kick my ass. But there was a 0 percent chance he could cuck me.

Trust me: No husband wants these guys fucking his wife. And no wife wants these losers fucking her.

They're *unexceptional*. They're no Roger Stones! They're not even Jerry Falwell Jr's!

Sometimes I wonder how it would play out though—if I invited one of these cuck-cursing hunks of nothing into our marital love dojo.[50]

You know, treat it like charity work. The first time Patriot Eagle has sex with a woman, I'm there, looming over the bed. My eyes locked on his.

He turns away from my gaze, but I'm still there. All there.

It's getting warm in our bedroom. But I make him keep that stupid red Make America Great Again hat on his head. His thermos of "Liberal Tears" empty.

"I may be a cuck, son," I whisper into his ear. I breathe for what feels like forever on his neck. "But I'm the motherfucking Alpha Cuck!"

---

50   "No," my wife says. "Delete this chapter."

25

CONSERVATIVES IN COMEDY

Why are there so few conservative comedians?

Because you can't support a family on an open-micer's salary.

Comedy is a tough gig. When you're starting out—especially in stand-up—you find yourself spending a lot. More than money, time. You're writing, getting up wherever you can, whenever you can. At some open mics you wait around for a couple hours for just a few minutes of stage time, where you get to try out material in front of other comics who are also waiting around for their turn. Some mics are free—others charge a cover and/or a drink minimum. Getting up, say, five nights a week adds up. Now imagine years of that—with no guarantee of a paying gig down the road.

I thought about this when we moved out of our one-bedroom apartment in Brooklyn Heights to a house in the country—a good hike from the City. We have yards now—a front one and a back one; a momma deer hides her baby under our deck in the back—and our basement is bigger than our apartment in BK was.

It took us some time to get used to the growth in our living space. The first few weeks in the house we kept to the rooms on the first floor. Sometimes it felt like other people must be living in the unoccupied rooms. Not in a poltergeist way. But in the way we would go weeks or even months in Brooklyn without hearing our neighbors. Many skipped town to wait out the pandemic in places like the home we were now getting used to.

One morning at around 3:30 AM we woke up to the loudest sound we had ever heard in our new part of the world. A spaceship was either landing or taking off in our basement. If I closed my eyes hard enough, a part of me thought, maybe it would just go away.

But it didn't go away. And it was up to me to go down there to meet whatever terrestrial had decided to make contact with us. Our toddler was asleep in the bedroom next to ours—his own room finally!—and my wife was pregnant with our new one. Both family members cute and useless for the task.

Unarmed, I crept downstairs, feeling around for the light switches on the walls I was still unfamiliar with. When I finally found them I saw that the sound was no alien but the water softener (whatever the hell that is) going haywire in the corner of the basement. And the sink across the room was overflowing with water, flooding our unfinished basement floor.

I didn't know what to do. I pulled the plug attached to the water softener, which stopped the cacophony but not the flood. I grabbed my phone—almost started live-tweeting about it—but had the mettle to hold back on sharing my quips and Googled "24-hour plumber" anywhere nearby.

There was one. I called the service, left a message, and a plumber called me back around 4:00 AM.

The sink was still overflowing and he wouldn't be able to make it out to us until later that morning. But until then at least he was able to help my useless ass shut off the water.

Check this out, new homeowners: There's a valve that reads "On" and "Off" with arrows showing you in which direction to turn it.

I managed to get back to sleep. I don't remember if my wife did. But our son miraculously slept through the whole ruckus.

When the plumber arrived, he took a look at the problem, and I paid him $106 to tell me he couldn't help me.

Later that day, I paid another guy $293.22 to empty my septic tank and another fella $373.19 to snake out the mainline from our house to the tank—which was the cause of the flooding. As the last septic man wrote out the invoice, I noticed the "Trump" sticker on the back of his pad.

Fuck, I thought. *I am in the wrong business.*

As I write this book, the plumber we hired to dig out and replace the old cast-iron pipe to the septic tank is now revamping the other pipes throughout the house: water, gas, and whatever the hell else happens behind these walls. His son is apprenticing.

We await the arrival of appliances that Plumber the Elder and Plumber the Younger will have to hook up for us. And I'm still thinking, *Fuck—I'm in the wrong business!* as I continue handing over checks to men who know the inner workings of my house and have other secret knowledge I do not possess: like when the fuck renovations will be done and my family can finally move back in. (I am typing this sentence at my in-laws', where we have been staying for the past three months. At night, my mother-in-law watches home-renovation reality shows—where every project is completed in an hour, including commercial breaks. She has no idea what she's doing to me.)

I don't know if any of the tradesmen I've been forking over my savings to have comedy aspirations or if they are even funny. But the guy who emptied my septic tank was a real inspiration. He seems to be living out a philosophy of work that I'm jealous of. In short: "If you want me to deal with your shit, you're gonna have to pay me."

That is far too often not the case with comedy. In fact, as I look back over my career, I was often the one paying to deal with other people's shit.

26

BOMBING

Bombing.

What normal person wants to risk that?

I'm lucky to have had some years of performing in front of live audiences under my belt before starting stand-up— well, getting up the nerve to finally give it a try. The thing about performing sketch or improv is that when things aren't going well, you're at least dying with other people. But when you're up there alone, you can feel like you're more than alone.

I remember it was my first stand-up performance of 2013. Not my first show ever. And it was in the back room of Amarachi Lounge in Bedford Stuyvesant, Brooklyn. The guy booking the gig had seen me some weeks back at a bar show on the Upper West Side. He told me that he wanted to see how I would do in front of "his people."

The night of the gig I had been battling hiccups for something like eight hours straight. They started on the set of a *Reservoir Dogs* parody Greg Burke and I had shot earlier that day for our YouTube channel, Greg and Lou.

I have no idea how many takes my hiccups ruined or if that kind of affliction was a good enough reason to pull out of a gig. In the outtakes video, which is also available on YouTube, Greg has a hiccup counter going. The camera has Greg framed in a closeup, tied to a chair, playing the poor cop in uniform who gets his ear cut off in Quentin Tarantino's 1991 flick.

I'm standing off-camera, reading my lines for Greg to respond to. We clocked eleven hiccups in that one take alone. I thought about bailing on the show that night—but I didn't. I had a gig—I said I'd be there, so I went. I hiccupped the whole subway ride over.

I was the comedy warm-up act for a night that was supposed to be part fashion-show, hip-hop performance—and maybe adult-toys sale?

I'm not sure. There were dildos and lubricants spread out on a coffee table in the billiards room.

I had shown up way too early. The show was never gonna start. And the only two other white people in the place were at the bar. White Dude #1 had a broken hand, which was being held together by what looked like torture pins. A bottle of Corona in his good hand, he was hitting on two Black women who had brought Popeyes Chicken to the lounge. The women, who were coincidentally offering massages in the same room as the dildos, were neglecting their mixed drinks so they could strip the chicken bones of their meat, both the dark and the white.

White Dude #2—the injured guy's friend or relative—was being a shitty wingman, sipping his beer soundlessly, while eyeing down the women like a man ready to be charged with something.

I wanted to bail—and was about to—when the audience was finally led in to the room where the stage was, and the host of the night, a man calling himself "Time of Your Life," introduced me to the room. Cold.

I don't think the audience was expecting an opening act. They were definitely not expecting me. I don't think they were ready for comedy. Apparently, I wasn't either.

I opened with an impromptu line about Mitt Romney that I can't remember, thankfully, because it was:

1) Not funny

2) A lame attempt to pander to the room

3) Dated

I followed up that piece-of-shit improvisation of good intentions with something that I actually thought would land:

"Man, I feel like President Obama up here," I said. "Because I have the opportunity to disappoint so many black people."

And disappoint I did. But not without a little help from this ditty of a follow-up:

"But no matter what happens here tonight, I would love to bring everyone back to my parents' house." Pause. "Because I want to see the look on their faces when I tell them I'm dating *all of you*."

…Yeah.

I was supposed to do ten minutes. I think I did seven. But I really hope it was five. Zero minutes would have been awesome.

I turned the mic back over to Time of Your Life—unaware at the time of the irony—and walked out of the room.

Apparently the PA system they were using fed into the main bar area, so the lounge's patrons got to hear me bomb.

But at least I got through my set without a literal hiccup. Although I must say—now that I'm remembering a sliver more of the set I did—that my porn observation—the one about black dudes always keeping their socks on when they fuck—did win the crowd over for a good part of a second. That moment came closest to any sort of "time of my life" for the night.

The event's organizer was nowhere in sight—thank God. But I mistakenly caught eyes with White Dude #1 and he said, "Good job."

I thanked the liar nonetheless and asked about his hand. "Long story," he said.

Of course it was. *Time of your life*, I bet.

The boxes from Popeyes were gone from the bar, as were the two ebony masseuses. I looked over at White Dude #2, who was just sitting there, lurking....

I'm thinking now of Ernest Hemingway's *A Movable Feast*, where Papa wrote what is possibly the greatest description of a man I have ever come across: "I tried to break his face down and describe it but I could only get the eyes. Under the black hat, when I had first seen them, the eyes had been those of an unsuccessful rapist."

I was gone before my hiccups started up again. By that time I think I had suffered through something like a day and a half of hiccupping.

For many comedians comedy can feel like years and years of hiccupping. You're sacrificing your time, money, and still chances are you will never have a career in this business.

Fortunately, now there are so many different avenues you can take in comedy—you may even end up writing a book about it—but even with all those avenues there is no guarantee you'll succeed.

Man, there's not even a guarantee you'll ever book a paying gig! Or at least one that will cover your travel expenses.

I once performed at a company's Christmas party. It was my first real paying gig. A sum agreed upon beforehand—not a "pass the hat"-after-the-show sort of thing.

The owner of the company had reserved the backroom of a restaurant in Manhattan. His staff was pretty diverse in terms of age. The roster was a mixture of what looked like young professionals and their grandparents. There was no stage. No microphone setup. And I was supposed to do twenty to thirty minutes of stand-up.

The year before the boss booked a mentalist to entertain his staff. This year—thanks to a college professor of mine, Barry Goldsmith, who had recommended me—I was the act.

Let's just say they should have brought back the mentalist.

I bombed so hard that I have blacked out that Christmas set from memory. But the pain lingers. I have a hard time dealing with silence—the natural lulls in the day when it's quiet in the country give me flashbacks.

What I do know is that when I was done with my set, I turned around and did a walk of shame away from the tables. I heard a few claps behind me—but maybe I'm making those up in post.

I had to wait around to be paid, you know. So I stood as far away from my audience as I could at the bar. The bartender was kind and helped me medicate with free drinks. A few of the company's employees came up to me. The young ones said it was a weird crowd. A couple old ones said…. Well, I don't know what they said.

What could they have possibly said to me at my own funeral?

In that moment I could really have used that white guy from the Bed Stuy gig. Just to hear, "Good job" again—even if it was another lie. Shit—I hurt so bad I could have even used his creepy friend just lurking around for the emotional support.

When the boss finally gave me the check—it was for $500—I felt like the right thing to do was to give it back. Or keep it—but quit comedy.

But somehow I found the resolve to keep it and live to bomb—and sometimes kill—another day.

I don't know how many normal people would make it through that. There are a lot more surefire ways to make a living in this world without being willing to humiliate yourself.

27

ACT LIKE YOU BELIEVE IT

Ladies, if your husband goes through gay-conversion therapy you know he's serious about your marriage.

Of course, you know he's still gay—but he is committed to the role. And that is worth something.

One night after my sketch group, the Hammerkatz, performed at the UCB Theater in Chelsea, Amy Poehler (one of the theater's founding members) was backstage.

"You guys really *commit*," she said. It was an amazing compliment for us young performers, just out of college, to receive—especially from a superstar like Poehler. And what was true in the early 2000s is still true today. You have to commit.

Whether you're playing a role on stage or in front of a camera, or putting on a persona in real life, the bedroom, or online—you have to act like you believe what you're saying. Especially if you're virtue signaling and/or trying to scare the shit out of people.

Over the last five-plus years there has been no shortage of fear mongers and doom-and-gloom pussies trying to whip others up. They're all over the place. But far too many of them just aren't acting like they truly believe what they're putting out there.

Below are some real examples of uncommitted role-playing.

ONE-IN-FIVE

I don't think girls should go to college. I know that sounds sexist. But trust me—it's coming from a good place. I am no member of the American Taliban.

Pre-COVID-19 I was horrified to hear that one-in-five female college students in the United States will be sexually assaulted on campus. One in five.

Horrific.

And I started thinking: *Wait, if one-in-five women will be sexually assaulted, why are parents letting their daughters go to college?*

Are parents insane?

And what about the people working for the colleges? Professors, administrators, recruiters—everybody! How the hell do you continue to work at an institution that allows this to happen?

Or maybe those numbers are bullshit? I sure hope so. Otherwise that means there are thousands of monsters who continue to draw a salary from institutions that prey upon young women.

Look, if I'm a Gender and Women's Studies professor, and out of the one hundred women in my Introduction to Simone de Beauvoir class you're telling me twenty of them will be sexually assaulted....

I'm gonna cancel that fucking class! Call the cops! Pull the fire alarm! Stand up at the podium and yell, "Ladies, get the fuck out of here! You are in danger!"

Think of all the politicians we have now, citing this statistic while at the same time pushing for legislation that would make college free. Why? So even more women go to college? More than half of college students are women already. Do these pols have any idea the message they're sending?

"Look, ladies, a fifth of you will suffer the trauma of sexual assault—but at least you won't be saddled with student loan debt on top of it!"

It's gruesome. But what is the answer?

I don't know. I used to think that if one-in-five women will be sexually assaulted on campus, maybe only four-in-five should go to college....

I'm sorry. I didn't major in math. Neither do many women. (I stand in solidarity with my non-STEM sisters.)

A possible solution might be found in what we learned during the pandemic, when for a time college classes were forced to go online. And while some say remote learning makes it harder for students to learn and connect with the material, it also makes it harder for them to be sexually assaulted. And that sounds like a silver lining to me. A very expensive—but also safer—silver lining.

IMMIGRATION

Be consistent. Even if you're consistently wrong.

Good or bad, I respect consistency. For example, I have a lot of respect for people who didn't pretend to care about immigrants under the Obama or Trump administrations.

Because pretending to care about immigrants depending on whether a Democrat or Republican is in the White House must be so stressful. Ultimately, your social media history—posts, likes, thumbnail filters—is going to out you.

So, how are you all holding up under the Biden administration? Are "kids in cages" or in "border facilities similar to jail"?

Immigration is a subject close to my heart—it's in my DNA after all. As you know, I am the son of an immigrant. My father came to the US in the 1970s, and in the 1980s he started a family and took over and grew a business. Throughout my life my father has taught me the value of hard work. That's why I plan on living off of his hard work for as long as I can.

Mi viejo's talking about retiring. But I've told him, "Wait a second, *Papí*. Let's see how my book sales go, then we can reassess the work situation."

I am thankful my father made that long journey over forty years ago and not a couple years ago under the Trump administration. Obviously if my father had tried to cross the border a few years ago he'd be in his 70s and I would have no chance of existing. I'm not talking about time-travel paradoxes—what I'm talking about is that Trump's America was not a hospitable place for people like my father—or so I was told every single day when 45 was in office.

Remember all the headlines, pundits, and blue-checks on Twitter calling Trump "Hitler" and comparing his administration and supporters to Nazis? Not a welcoming look.

But the same people who were calling Trump Hitler also wanted to let migrants and asylum seekers into the country. It didn't make sense—all this mixed messaging. What American in his right mind would ever let immigrants—legal, undocumented, or refugee—enter the country while Hitler was in office?

But even with our Hitler in Chief occupying the White House, foreigners still wanted in!

It is truly a testament to how amazing our country is that Donald Trump was president and people were still risking their lives to get here.

Celebrities on the other hand were threatening to leave. That's right—*celebrities*! The people with the cushiest lives imaginable. Lives so privileged they have to stage their own hate crimes.

If living under a Trump dictatorship would be too hard for Lena Dunham to bear, can you imagine what life was going to be like for María, a single mother with two children fleeing a murderous drug cartel in Central America?

Celebs like Dunham said they wanted out—but, of course, they didn't leave. Why would they? They could openly mock Hitler right here in the good old US-of-A without fear for their safety or social repercussions.

If celebrities had really cared, we should have seen them down at the border, *building* The Wall, pleading with the throngs of wretched Latin Americans to: "Stay out, María! It's not safe here! You can't nanny our children or clean our mansions!...Not right now. Check back in 2020. Biden might have this."

And Biden did have this. He won the 2020 presidential election and those folks from south of the border looking for a better life got the message. Even with Vice President Kamala Harris telling them, "Don't come"—the border has been flooded. And not with celebrities returning home from self-exile during the Trump years.

FASCISM

I would only take your "Trump is Hitler" sign seriously if you owned a gun. And your gun(s) should be featured prominently in the same picture as the sign. I think that's what "common-sense gun control" should mean: If Hitler is in the White House you better be armed.

But gun-control organizations like Everytown and Moms Demand Action, as well as antigun activists and members of Congress, were still pushing their version of common sense—that is, disarming US citizens—which, under the circumstances, sounded fucking suicidal.

Speaking as a proud American, if I'm going to commit suicide I want it be by my own hand—not the government's.

(Statistically speaking that is how it's most likely to go down: self-inflicted. But knowing me, I'm more likely to perish via autoerotic asphyxiation—not firearm suicide. Unless I happen to forget to empty the chamber before sticking the gun up my ass.)

In addition to dealing with Hitler we had mass shootings, school shootings, riots, arson, and warlords taking over whole city blocks, declaring them "autonomous zones." Scary stuff.

So scary in fact, I thought, "Now is not the time to have a national conversation on gun control." Because everything I was seeing—and everything everybody with a platform was saying—screamed, "Lou! Get! A! Gun!"

Stephen Colbert devoted his show to taking on President Trump. But if Colbert and his comrades in late-night really wanted me to believe that *they* believed Trump was a fascist, instead of talking gun control, they should have been talking militias. Specifically how they can start one.

Imagine all the crossover potential. We could have seen episodes of *The Late Show* with Stephen Colbert and *The Late Late Show* with James Corden, where the hosts do cheesy musical numbers about their weapons training, Corden does carpool karaoke in a tank, and they bring in Samantha Bee to discuss how they plan on breaching the entrance to the Oval Office should Trump refuse to leave office. Jimmy Fallon's giggling—like he always does—but this time he's quoting Thomas Jefferson: "'The tree of liberty must be refreshed from time to time with the blood of patriots and tyrants'... We'll be right back with Ariana Grande!"

Trump made it four years in office without one host stepping up to be the Claus von Stauffenberg of late-night.

They may have called Trump a fascist, a dictator, and Hitler—but, like so many role-players, they didn't act like they believed it.

CLIMATE CHANGE

Not like any of this matters. We are facing extinction right here and right now. So I hear.

Climate Change.

Climate Crisis.

Climate Emergency.

Climate [INSERT REALLY BAD WORD].

The problem is, as I've been saying, all the people telling me I should be scared about climate change aren't acting scared enough.

The world is gonna end in twelve years and you're taking another improv class? (At a theater you accuse of systemic oppression and white supremacy?)

If you say you're scared, could you please start *acting* scared? Commit!

Where are all the liberal doomsday preppers? All the preppers I've seen are conservatives. If you want me to take you seriously—I don't know—start stockpiling kombucha? Learn homeopathic emergency medical procedure! Prep it up!

If you believe The Flood is coming—act like The Flood is coming! Buy a pair of swim wings, Millennial Noah!

Especially if you're a politician or celebrity. Leonardo DiCaprio's foundation may have raised $100 million to save the planet—but I'm not impressed. The dude is loaded. What is money to him?

If Leo really wants me to listen, he should stop flying his private jet all over the world to have sex with supermodels.

Actually, if the world is ending, sex with supermodels sounds pretty good.

But if he sincerely cares about the environment, he'll stop burning fossil fuels for travel and stick to making love to locally sourced free-range supermodels.

One-hundred million dollars might offset his carbon footprint—but it's not making a dent in his carbon dickprint.

Don't get me wrong—I believe in climate change. I'm just not going to pretend that it frightens me. The same people who say "follow the science" don't think science will find a way to handle a few more degrees on the planet. And those same people almost never talk about building new nuclear power plants—which would have a real impact on climate change, as well as being a safe, dependable, and efficient source of energy.

Instead, while nuclear power plants are being decommissioned around the country, late-night hosts came together in September of 2021 for one night of comedy focused on climate change.

But it wasn't enough to change the planet or to win over critics at *Gizmodo* who lamented:

1) Jimmy Fallon didn't host a "*Hot Ones* segment [where guests eat spicy food]. Too bad, it would've been a perfect chance to sit down with noted climate guy and Southerner Al Gore or perhaps Stacey Abrams or even guest Jane Goodall."

2) Jimmy Kimmel "messed up words from the teleprompter—he said 'wild flires' at one point, and did a serious stumble over the 'IPCC' ('I can't even say their name, that's how serious it is'). Seems like someone isn't really used to talking about climate."

3) James Corden's bits: "Not exactly the stuff of systemic change needed."

Now, I am not in public relations or marketing—especially when it comes to the Big Fear industry. But a world that produces the kind of "entertainment" described above is a world not worth saving!

If you are looking to persuade people to save the planet you should look back to 2017, when Hurricane Irma blasted Florida.

At the time police had to warn Floridians not to shoot their guns at the storm. And everyone laughed at those trigger-happy idiots, when they should have been listening to those trigger-happy idiots.

Because Florida Man shooting bullets at a hurricane might be only a little less effective than a jet-setting multimillionaire paying for carbon offsets or network late-night hosts producing cringe climate propaganda.

But emptying a magazine at the weather?—now that is what Act-Like-You-Believe-It looks like! And goddamn, it is way more entertaining!

28

ACTIVIST COMEDIAN

When it comes to comedy the only change I can hope to effect in the world is to make an audience laugh. It's a small thing, I know: They weren't laughing—but now they are. And that, ladies and gentlemen, is enough for me....

But to be fair: It's not like I'm a celebrity. I don't have fuck-you money. No one has ever asked me to sing John Lennon's "Imagine." There is no telling how much of a self-important douchebag I would become if I was even just a little bit important. (With your help though, maybe one day we can put *me* to the test.)

In the meantime I have to contend with the real possibility that I wouldn't make a good activist to begin with. Maybe I'd end up hurting whatever cause I'm pushing.

I've known so many unlikeable people who have volunteered for political campaigns and ballot propositions. They're knocking on doors, phone banking—now they're texting you!—and all I'm thinking is, *I might vote the other way just to hurt you!*

How many votes do you think have been cast as "Fuck yous" to celebrities who use their platforms to sermonize instead of entertain?

How far would you go to stick it to that know-it-all from high school who keeps updating her thumbnail on Facebook with whatever *cause du jour* is trending?

In 2017 comedian Jeremy McLellan wrote a piece for *Cato Unbound*'s "The Very Serious Comedy Issue" titled "Bombing on Stage: Comedy as Political Resistance." In it McLellan uses the story of Saint Genesius of Rome to illustrate the comedian's fear of "being murdered for insulting the room."

In the same issue I responded to his essay with my own: "A Different Comedy Nightmare," where I describe a fear of mine that lies at the opposite end of the spectrum with the tortured and beheaded patron saint of comedians. I'm talking about the safe, very nonmartyred comedian who, instead of slinging legit jokes, spends his stage time preaching to the choir—whichever choir that may be.

As I perform for more libertarians like myself, a fear has crept in—a nightmare that I pray to Saint Genesius never materializes:

> *It's a packed house—made up mostly of male libertarian undergrads in ill-fitting suits—but not as many of them are wearing bow ties as you'd expect.*
>
> *I'm on stage, mic in hand, working through my material.*
>
> *Everyone's applauding….*
>
> *But no one is laughing.*
>
> *My entire set, I get nothing but clapter.*

I'm telling you, when you are up on that stage, finally in a room full of people who think like you do—especially when your view of the world puts you in the minority—you can feel righteous. Forget about being an activist—you can feel almost messianic, like the patron saint of liberty!

It. Is. Tempting.

"To answer their calling," as McLellan puts it so eloquently in his essay, "comedians must assert their independence and resist becoming either soothing court jesters to the powerful or propagandists for activist causes. As artists, the temptations of Leviathan are hard to resist, as are those of its opponents."

Being a libertarian has made it easier for me to eschew the party line(s) and flex my own righteousness by holding up a mirror to the State, as well as to its actors, supporters, and clowns. But something I try to remember to do is to turn that mirror around every now and then and examine myself and my side.

I know sometimes I am preaching to the choir, but I am happy to be part of the congregation. At this point in my membership, I experience a lot more laughs than clapter.

And I don't fear that I will suffer the same fate as Genesius. These are different times, of course. But also it is much harder to behead a libertarian, because we're liable to be armed with an AR-15.

29

LIBTARD

What upsets libertarians about the Holocaust?

That it was carried out by the state and not the free market.

Feel free to redistribute my joke to those in need of it.

I am a libertarian comedian—or a comedian who happens to be a libertarian. Whichever works for you.

I've opened for Ron Paul. I've attended The Porcupine Freedom Festival, and spoken at Liberty Forum and other events for the Free State Project—all in the "Live Free or Die" state of New Hampshire.

At one of my gigs a college kid wearing his father's suit asked me to sign a copy of the US Constitution and a high schooler had me autograph Henry Hazlitt's *Economics in One Lesson*—both signatures happened only hours apart.

I am so libertarian that I once took part in an event called "Laughing for Liberty: The Role of Comedy in Politics" for members of Young Americans for Liberty, at William Jewell

College in…*Liberty*, Missouri. That is some liberty overkill right there. We could really use a new word.

Most people don't know what a libertarian is. I was the first libertarian my wife had ever met. I'm guessing I was the first one she ever slept with too.[51]

One thing about being a libertarian is that no matter what happens in an election, we're going to be unhappy—and I'm not just talking about bringing about the End Times—or in the colloquial: helping a Republican win.

There is a certain *liberty* in that never-ending unhappiness and struggle with the state—to be natural outsiders to the political process. To always be "punching up"—if you will—at the powers that be. Whichever party that may be.

We're also weirdos: libertarians. That's why I want us to appropriate the word "libtard." Not because I've been called a libtard way more times than I've been called a cuck. But because I think it makes more sense to call me a libtard than it does to call your run-of-the-mill liberal or progressive one. Because I have been and still am a retard for liberty.

The night before the 2016 general election I performed stand-up comedy at Gary Johnson's last campaign stop at the House of Blues in San Diego, California. I went up early in the lineup.

"Unfortunately, I can't stick around," I told the libertarians in attendance. "Because I have to hop a flight back to New York, so I can vote for Gary Johnson."

The crowd cheered.

"Because we all know if I don't vote for him there is no way he's gonna win New York."

They laughed. I finished my set—had a great time. Caught my flight back to New York without a hiccup and

---

51   Sorry, boys. Submissions to join Alpha Cuck and his señora in their bedroom are closed.

cast my ballot for Gary Johnson and Bill Weld—the Libertarian Party candidates who hadn't even bothered to show up to their campaign event the night before.

Their absence wasn't out of the ordinary—this is the LP we're talking about—but Trump winning was unthinkable. I had so many sketch ideas ready to welcome our first Madam President. Trump fucked it all up.

I walked into Custom House on Montague Street in Brooklyn Heights and took a seat at the bar. The TVs were tuned to either CNN or MSNBC. I started drinking as the election results continued to come in.

The place was packed and in a panic. I remember so many men wearing scarves indoors—constricting their necks as the world they knew was falling apart. I drank in the madness of it all and chased it with alcohol.

I woke up naked the next morning on my couch. My clothes were scattered all over my apartment.

I checked the time on my phone and remembered…"Oh shit—I missed my flight!"

That's right—this libtard had flown from San Diego to New York—to vote for candidates who had no shot of winning office and who had skipped their own campaign event—only to have to fly back to Los Angeles the following day for another gig.

Libtard.

It cost me like $700 to buy a new plane ticket and I rushed over to Newark *Liberty* International Airport to sweat out my hangover.

I was miserable. But my sickness was a bodily matter—it would go away eventually. The sickness of my Brooklyn neighbors though—that was a spiritual matter. Because with Trump in office there could be no God.

Looking back, perhaps the hangover and hit to my pocket were my punishment for the sin of voting third-party.

30

I AM BECOME DEATH

If you want to know what it feels like to murder, vote third-party in a US presidential election.

When Donald Trump won in 2016, not only did Democrats blame third-party voters like myself for his victory, but also they charged that we were complicit in the inevitable bloodbath that was to come during the reign of POTUS 4-5.

Mind you, I voted Libertarian in New York, a state that Hillary Clinton was incapable of losing.[52] And yet somehow, the carnage on the horizon was my fault.

Funny how that same election calculus doesn't work when their guy wins a four-year stay in the White House. I have yet to hear any Obama voters apologize for the blood his administration shed. But, I guess, if it's on me to apologize for Trump, then I have to apologize for Obama too, whom

---

52   Trump may have said, "I could stand in the middle of Fifth Avenue and shoot somebody, and I wouldn't lose any voters, okay?" But that's bullshit—Hillary is the candidate who could pull that off. Forget about losing votes, she would gain them—in New York, for sure.

I voted for in 2008. Those four years of Hope, Change, and Death—that's on me, guys.

But don't hang any of the Dubya years on me—I didn't vote in 2000, and in 2004 I voted for John Kerry. I don't want to hear any of your bullshit about Joe Biden either. That's on *you*.[53]

It was one thing to see people I didn't know (or care to know) on social media call third-party voters traitors and ridicule us for exercising our right to say, "Nuh-uh," to the two major parties. It was another thing to have someone I actually knew reach out to damn us directly.

That was one hell of an email you sent, Brad!

Granted, I didn't really know Brad. I had only met him once. My wife and I had dinner with him and his boyfriend. Brad was in his sixties, long-retired from practicing law, and his boyfriend, Bradley[54], was younger by probably a decade, handsome, and worked in healthcare. Both were "With Her."

The night started at Brad's house in West Hollywood, where he showed my wife and me his art collection. Some guys build man caves, Brad built a man gallery. We talked about a recent visit to The Getty Museum, where a security guard recognized me from my YouTube videos.

"Do you get recognized a lot?" Brad said.

"Not enough," I said.

It made more sense for us to carpool over to the restaurant—parking being what it is in Los Angeles. We took Brad's Tesla. It was my first time in the luxury electric car brand. I could barely hear the engine, and the drive over felt more like floating.

---

53 Not every *you*. You know who *you* are.

54 I have changed the names of the real-life couple, but not the relationship of their names to each other. They had the same name, as if parents have so few options when naming their gay sons.

Sharing a table with Brad and Bradley, these two wealthy, healthy, cultured gay men, I felt inadequate. I always feel that way when hanging out with gay couples. Throughout the meal, I thought, *My wife and I must be boring the shit out of these guys.*

I'm sure we could have made things interesting, but my wife is such a cockblock.

We never had a second double-date though. Never rode in Brad's Tesla again (the ride back to his house from dinner was our last time). Never saw his art collection again either—who knows what new pieces he's added to it?

It's hard enough scheduling those kinds of dates. Now add politics into the mix—the 2016 existential election at that!—and oh boy!

Voting third-party was an abomination, and Brad's email read like a curse he was putting upon me and my third and fourth generations to come. Brad was particularly concerned about the deaths of trans people that I was now party to.

Look—I take full responsibility for the people I have murdered and will murder. But this? Third-party voter, six-hundred-thousand-degrees-of-separation murder? I don't think I can sign the confession for that. I won't even admit to manslaughter.

I wonder though—by Brad's logic—would I be responsible for all the deaths of trans people during the Trump years? The suicides and the homicides? What about the homicides committed by significant others or, in the case of trans sex workers, their johns?

If I have blood on my hands I want to know the exact details of how that blood got there. Because I am happy to live in a time where trans adults are able to get the medical care they need—without having to buy medicine from shady drug dealers or having to resort to self-harm because they are denied gender-affirming surgery.

(Plus, when it comes to comedy, we can finally put to bed the whole "Are women funny?" debate. Because Eddie Izzard is definitive proof that they are.)

I never responded to Brad's email. I didn't like his tone, you know. And I try to keep my social circle to people who haven't accused me of murder. But I do wonder: How many deaths is Brad responsible for?

Because one of the problems in the LGBTQ+ community is that it's not really a "community" at all. So much discrimination exists between the groups. For example, there is tension between lesbians and trans women—in particular the trans women who try to shame lesbians as bigots for not wanting to suck their cocks. (Ironically, that seems like such a straight-guy move.)

On the other side are gay men who don't fully accept trans men—at least as lovers. The gay men I know love cock—not pussy. My closest homosexuals are all flaming gold-star gays, in that they have never had sex with women.

I don't care how many women Brad's had sex with. He grew up in a time when it was difficult to come out—I'm sure he broke a few ingenues' hearts in the small town where he grew up before coming out to the West Coast.

No, what I want to know is how many trans men has Brad been with? The two Brads—toss Bradley in there too, while we're at it.

Ever bottom for a trans man, boys? Let them strap on a dildo and give it to you—in solidarity with trans activism?

Have you ever given it to *them*—treated them like the petite hunks of masculinity that they are? Tom from Finland—but with a pussy!

Sex speaks louder than words—much louder than voting. If you truly believe in something, act like you believe it—and go ahead and fuck it!

Show him your art collection! Give him a ride in your Tesla! Show the (trans) man a good time!

His life is in your hands too. Why not his pussy?

Unless he voted third-party, of course. If so, then fuck that self-hating murderer.[55]

---

55   Figuratively.

31

NO FUCKS GIVEN

It's not that I don't give a fuck. It's that I give a fuck about different things. So, if you happen to catch me in a state of "no fucks given" that's probably what's happening. I think that's the case with most people who are applauded for "not giving a fuck."

Sometimes not giving a fuck isn't even a conscious choice—it's just a reality of our brain's limited bandwidth. It's like Dunbar's number—except instead of limiting the number of people "with whom one can maintain stable social relationships," it's limiting the number of *causes* with which one can maintain stable honest relationships.

You can only care so much about so much, before you're just pretending.

I had this epiphany—if you want to call it that; I'll call it that—back in college, during my Belief and Skepticism course with Professor Mark Cohen.

One day in class I raised my hand and declared, "I don't care about Africa."

Okay—I definitely need to clarify a few things.

1) I was raising my hand to be called upon by my professor—I wasn't doing a Nazi salute.

2) My statement was germane to the conversation we were having in class. Because how weird would it have been if out of nowhere I just blurted out, "I don't care about Africa!"?

3) I was really buff at the time, working out like a maniac—these were during my glory days of free modeling with baby oil—and I still spoke with a thick Queens/Long Island accent. So, I understand hearing "I don't care about Africa" coming out of that mouth, with that body, and with that accent probably sounded like a hate crime.

4) Fortunately, Professor Cohen fostered a learning environment where we could have difficult conversations like this one, and he gave me the opportunity to explain my position, which was pretty simple: How can I say I care about Africa if I'm not doing anything for Africa?

I noted that I, like my aghast classmates, was sitting in a classroom on NYU's Greenwich Village campus—we weren't over there in the motherland helping people. All this "caring" was just lip service. These were the days before you could change your thumbnail filters on Facebook to show support. Actually, these were the days when Facebook was still just a Harvard thing.

I don't remember where the class discussion went from there, but Professor Cohen said that my position was "interesting."

I'll take it.

I will have you know that since that day I have had moments of giving a fuck about Africa. You can tell, because I kept the receipts. Thanks to Gret Glyer's giving platform, DonorSee, I have helped poor individuals on the continent feed babies, build a chicken farm, and dig wells, among other things I've given a fuck about.[56]

DonorSee is the only website where you will never regret making drunken impulse purchases. One night you have a few too many drinks, blackout, and when you finally come to in the morning you see that you've fully funded the purchase of a prosthetic leg for a one-legged child in Malawi.

So, what do you *really* give a fuck about?

---

56   I have also made a one-time donation to Operation Smile. I give a fuck
     a few bucks at a time.

32

HATER[57]

Years ago I attended a debate between Christopher Hitchens and Dinesh D'Souza. This was around the time Hitch's book *God Is Not Great: How Religion Poisons Everything* came out, and D'Souza was still the president of King's College.

I forget the motion they were debating—something having to do with religion, of course. Those were the days of the New Atheists debating theists all over the country. It was during this period that it really hit me: If we are able to argue over religion and the existence of God, then no subject—and no faith—is off-limits.

I was a strident atheist at the time. I've mellowed out since then—I even have what I refer to as my crises of *no-faith*—but I have not taken any sacred cows, in that I still believe when it comes to debate and especially when

---

57 A version of this chapter was first published in *Spiked* as "In defence of 'hate speech.'"

it comes to comedy that it's all fair game. If anything, the invention of new sacred cows—as laid down in woke scripture—is an open invitation for mockery and profanity.

Today so many comedians abide by the new rules and end up delivering the same punch lines. Even "outsiders" like Trevor Noah and John Oliver are spewing the same opinions just with different accents.

The New Atheists didn't introduce me to this blasphemous mode of thinking—George Carlin was already one of my gods—but they definitely helped strengthen it for me. And the terrorist attack on *Charlie Hebdo* radicalized me.

The January 7, 2015, murders of staff members of the French satirical newspaper for the sin of publishing cartoons of Islam's Prophet Muhammad didn't inspire me to join in the fun by becoming an Islamic jihadist—no, I instead became a free-speech jihadi.

For every radical like myself who condemned the murders there were just as many, if not more, religious and secular turds proclaiming, "I believe in free speech, *but...* [INSERT LINE TO NEGATE THE FIRST PART OF THIS SENTENCE]."

A dozen lives were taken and eleven others injured at *Charlie Hebdo* and yet you'd hear about the paper's racism and its "punching down" on Muslims—if not to justify the attack, then at least to acknowledge its causality. You know, the whole "Those satirists knew what they were doing—what did they expect?"

Of course, what *Charlie Hebdo* did was not "punching down." Satirizing Islam is actually "punching up." Because there is no God but Allah, and Muhammad is His messenger (Peace be upon Him). You can't punch up—or blaspheme—higher than *That*. Calling it "hate speech" does not change that universal truth.

* * *

When I started out in comedy, I never thought, *One day, Lou, if you work hard enough, develop your craft, and keep grinding...you'll be defending "hate speech."*

But the reality is if you're going to be a free-speech jihadi you're gonna have to defend the "hate speech." It can suck at times. You proclaim to the world, "I may not agree with what you have to say, but I will defend to the death your right to say it."

Then someone says something and you're like, "Oh c'mon, man! You're gonna make me die for *that*?"

What is an obvious principle to me is not so obvious to the rest of the world or to my countrymen here in the States, unfortunately. Even though other countries attempt (and fail) to legislate the hate away, the US Supreme Court has consistently upheld constitutional protections for even the speech that we hate.

That's why in 2018–2019 I produced a minidocumentary for We the Internet TV called *Five Reasons Why We Need Hate Speech*. I know the title is cheeky clickbait—"Are you really telling us decent human beings that we *need* hate speech? Are you serious, asshole?"

But the goal of the minidoc was to show how the very hate speech laws and speech codes being pushed—often by the those on the Left—to protect the most vulnerable and marginalized are bound to be used against the most vulnerable and marginalized.

The video came out at a time when controversial—"extremist"—figures like Milo Yiannopoulos, Alex Jones, and Louis Farrakhan were being banned from platforms like Facebook.

It's easy to look the other way when those you despise are being silenced, but principles dictate you speak up even for those guys.[58]

Although I feel like a throwback to a different era, at least I'm in good company. I got help from the former national president of the American Civil Liberties Union, Nadine Strossen, and Pulitzer-Prize winning journalist Glenn Greenwald. Both appear in the documentary.

Spoiler alert: "hate-speech" laws, as Strossen points out in her book *Hate: Why We Should Resist It with Free Speech, Not Censorship*, "consistently have been enforced to suppress unpopular views and speakers, including political dissent and minority speakers."

No matter the platform—be it social media, or a college campus, or even an entire continent like "enlightened" Europe—hate-speech regulations lead to abuse, confusion, and growing numbers of people weaponizing the regulations as a form of vigilante justice to shut down speakers, end careers, and even justify real violence.

That's because hate speech is whatever you want it to be, baby. It has no specific definition. That is why such disparate figures as respected academic Camille Paglia and alt-right Richard Spencer—not to mention conservative Ben Shapiro, philosopher Christina Hoff Sommers, and the ACLU's Claire Guthrie Gastañaga—have all been branded preachers of hate. The term has become a catch-all for any speech that anyone hates, whether it's virulent white nationalism or reasoned social commentary defending civil liberties.

When I was with We the Internet TV, I blasphemed for a living. After all, if you don't offend some audiences, do you even *satire*, bro?

---

58   I'll have you know, Louis Farrakhan is one of my least-favorite Lou's.

That means I was frequently bumping up against the self-appointed censors of social media with their ever-updating algorithms and metastasizing free-speech codes. Facebook, like a member of the European Union, was particularly active in trying to root out hate speech during my tenure at WTI. Which means it was targeting just about everyone.

Were you ever "Zucced"? That is, suspended from the platform when your posts run afoul of Facebook CEO Mark Zuckerberg's community standards.

In Facebook jail, you're forced to spend time in the real world without the ability to check Facebook! (Which made me wonder: *When you're allowed back on, do you have to do the digital version of going door-to-door, informing neighbors on your feed that their posts are being "liked" by a hate-speech offender?*)

At the time I never thought it could happen to me. But then Facebook struck down a WTI post, because it went against Facebook's "community standards on hate speech."

So, I guess, this is my version of going door-to-door.

What was the hateful speech in question?

A poll, in which I asked, "Whose fault is Hurricane Florence?"

This was back in 2018, when the bastards at the World Meteorological Organization decided to name the tropical cyclone "Florence," after my mother.

More than 16,000 Facebook users weighed in before FB prematurely closed the poll. Of those who responded, 25 percent blamed the weather event on "Donald Trump."

The other 75 percent blamed "The Gays."

Because those were the only two choices I gave them.

I know it's never good when you have to explain a joke—and I'm sure you got it the first time—but, considering hate is on the line, here it goes:

In September of 2018, the *Washington Post* ran a headline claiming President Trump "is complicit" in hurricanes. It reminded me of evangelical preachers in recent memory who had blamed hurricanes on gay people.[59] We've seen so many hurricanes since Florence. Will the gays ever stop?

I still lean towards the principle that Facebook is free to censor whomever and whatever it wants. Zuckerberg may once have called his product "the digital equivalent of the town square," but it's still—for the time being—his sovereign platform to regulate. And the platform is dying because of the way he's regulating it.

For those who want to see the government step in and legislate Facebook and the other social-media platforms, did you ever watch those congressional hearings where Zuckerberg and his fellow Silicon Valley villains took questions from our elected inquisitors who had no fucking idea what they were talking about?

They were the sorts of questions your cute grandparents with dementia might ask—"Honey, do you have a google on you?"—but they have no business being anywhere near crafting legislation for the internet.[60] They're liable to get caught in a phishing scam.

Whether it's the state or corporate actors—or a state/corporate partnership (you know, fascism)—you become pretty skeptical of a censor's good intentions when it's your "hate speech" they're censoring.

---

59 Before heading out each morning, I still ask my gay neighbor whether I should take an umbrella.

60 Now imagine every other congressional committee. They are all packed with representatives who have no clue what they are doing.

At the time I thought if allegations of hate speech can be wielded to make even a well-meaning comedic post disappear, what else and who else can they remove?

Well, we all know. The same people who blamed Big Tech for getting Trump elected in 2016 praised those same corporations for booting The Donald off their platforms in the lead-up to the 2020 election.

*   *   *

Four years since my fateful gay weather-related poll was removed from Facebook, things have only gotten worse on the platform. It's kind of funny.

During the times of COVID I have noticed a shift away from hate-speech demerits to the removal of misinformation and forcing COVID-19 disclaimers onto posts that happen to even graze the topic.

"Turns out the COVID vaccine did NOT sterilize me," I wrote in one post. "WTF! Now I have to pay for my vasectomy! Fuck you, Bill Gates!"

Facebook reassured my followers and friends who read my joke that "COVID-19 vaccines go through many tests for safety and effectiveness and are then monitored closely." Their source: the World Health Organization.[61]

"I knew the vaccine would save lives," I wrote in another post. "But I never thought it would also reveal the people who want you dead."

In response to that, Facebook recommended my readers "Visit the COVID-19 Information Center for vaccine resources."

---

61   FYI: I remain fertile. At least I think so.

"In 2020 it was 'You just want to kill grandma!'" I noted on my wall. "But in 2021 it became 'We just want to kill unvaccinated grandma!'"

Before a fan of mine was allowed to share that post to his wall, Facebook popped up to give him a "Make sure you're sharing reliable information" nudge.

Facebook's rapid-test algorithm picked up the above examples, but let the following one pass:

> "Don't worry. The Omega variant will be the
> last variant."[62]

I had no idea my post was *not* misinformation. Maybe I'm a prophet.

* * *

It is easy to blame the algorithm or the programmers who write the code.

I used to think the problem was that a computer—unlike human beings—isn't nuanced enough to determine what is "hate speech" or misinformation—and definitely not sophisticated enough to know comedy.

But, as my 2-percent Neanderthal ass continues to interact with online *homo sapiens*, I have to admit: when it comes to mimicking human beings the algorithm isn't all the way there yet—but it is mighty close.

62　It should be, right? What do they do when they run out of Greek letters? Start over from alpha or leap to another language?

33

LETTER FROM A COWARD

One of the consequences of cancel culture is the chilling effect it has on speech. As many public intellectuals have pointed out, we hear all about the people who've been fired or deplatformed for what they've said—or for what people have been told they've said. After all, there is no entrance exam to join a protest mob. How else can you explain monuments to abolitionists being given the same vandal's treatment as the statues of slaveholders?

No, we may hear a lot about those who were willing to put their thoughts out there and were punished for it, but we don't hear about the people who look at the playing field and decide, "You know what—saying what's on my mind just isn't worth the risk."

I know polling has been done on the subject—and the results aren't looking good—but I knew that already. I have had firsthand experience with this *chill* over the years.

Members of the "silent majority" hit me up to confess their thought crimes. I'm really easy to get in touch with. Probably too easy—and way too eager to talk. They trust me—which is something I'm proud of. Almost always it's the same spiel: "I haven't changed. I'm still liberal. But now I worry I'm not allowed to say what I think—to say what was totally acceptable to think and say five minutes ago!"

I know people who enjoy the work I'm doing, but are afraid to like or share it publicly, because they fear possible backlash. In a time where even the smallest disagreement can be costly, who wants to disagree or share the work of a disagreeable funny man like me?

I get messages like this one:

"Sorry that I am a coward. I typed a comment on your Bernie post but didn't go through with it for fear that somebody I work with might see it and ding me for being unenlightened."

I wasn't sure which Bernie post of mine the coward was referring to. I've made a lot of them. My favorite one is about how much I love to hear Bernie speak, because he always sounds like he's giving the sloppiest blowjob. (He does, doesn't he? And it's one of those BJ's where there's way too much spit—so you can't even feel it. You know what I'm talking about?)

Well, I can understand why someone would abstain from commenting on that very unenlightened post of mine.

But it turns out the post the coward was referring to was one I had written in response to an opinion piece I read in the *San Francisco Chronicle* about Bernie Sanders's attire at the 2021 presidential inauguration.

The US Senator from Vermont wore a blue mask, puffy jacket, and mittens. The mittens were showstoppers, and all together his getup birthed the great Bernie Sanders mittens meme. You know the one, where Bernie is sitting slouched in a chair, looking miserable under his surgical mask, with his legs and arms crossed.

In the days following the peaceful transfer of power, while half the country was celebrating the Biden/Harris victory and a sizable percentage of self-described patriots were still trying to Stop the Steal, all Americans were united in the pure enjoyment of seeing Bernie Sanders and his mittens photoshopped into every scene imaginable. From *Game of Thrones* to Georges Seurat's *A Sunday Afternoon on the Island of La Grande Jatte* to Bernie arm-barring a mixed-martial artist in the UFC Octagon, the mitten memes still hold up.

Of course, whatever brings you joy, whatever's fun, whatever is apolitical, you can be sure there is somebody out there ready to ruin it in 800 words or less. That's what think pieces are really—thinking up new ways to force one writer's misery onto others. And so it was in that article published in the *San Francisco Chronicle* titled "S.F. high school students get a lesson in subtle white privilege."

"Where could this possibly be going?" you might ask.

"I mean in no way to overstate the parallels," Ingrid Seyer-Ochi, a high school teacher writes. "Sen. Sanders is no white supremacist insurrectionist. But he manifests privilege, white privilege, male privilege and class privilege, in ways that my students could see and feel."

Yeah. The old socialist Jew wore mittens, so, obviously whatever Ingrid said.

At least if Ingrid were being honest she would have changed that last sentence to something like: "But he manifests privilege, white privilege, male privilege and class privilege, in ways that [I have indoctrinated] my students [to] see and feel."

Her article reminds me of what it was like to major in the humanities in college. You have a paper due the next day and you haven't written anything. So what do you do? Easy: analyze the subject matter through a Marxist lens or give it a Marxist-Feminist reading, bang out the thousand words you need, turn it in, and get your B-minus.

Ingrid's opinion isn't even worth a B-minus! Check out this sentence of hers: "I puzzled and fumed as an individual as I strove to be my best possible teacher." Forget about green-lighting the piece, what editor let this piece-of-shit line through?

In his book *The Painted Word*, Tom Wolfe rips on modern art, describing how things have gone from "seeing is believing" to "believing is seeing." The same thing is going on here. There is no privilege in Bernie's mittens to be seen—but if you want to believe there is, you can trick your mind into seeing it. You can trick your mind into seeing anything.

If you want to know what real privilege looks like it's being able to get bullshit like this published in the *San Francisco Chronicle*—this wasn't even a post on Medium!—and having a grown-ass man be too much of a coward to call it out.

Now I know I've chosen a different path—I don't have "enlightened" co-workers whom I risk offending when pointing out the obvious. Years ago, I made the conscious decision that I would never be employable. I'm all in on this comedy game! You don't have to be. But unless you are willing to speak up, you have to—at the very least—support those of us who are.

I'm no hero. I'm no coward either. My DMs are open.

NO APOLOGIES

Why would anyone ever apologize today?

There's no upside to it. You see so many people who issue public apologies, only to lose jobs, future prospects, and their dignity.

At least when I apologize to my wife, she has sex with me. But there's no make-up sex with the public.

Most of the time the people you're apologizing to have never even paid for your work. Your acts of contrition are yet more free content for the sadists.

That's why I say, don't apologize to people you don't respect for things you're not sorry for.

But if you are thinking of apologizing, at the very least ask to see some receipts. And sex.

35

RADIOACTIVE

I didn't set out to do political comedy. But you go where the gigs take you. With We the Internet TV, I started out as a freelance contributor and then became head writer and executive producer. Later, I dropped the "executive" in my title and just went with producer. I still don't know the difference between a producer and an executive producer—but I do know that I was responsible for taking on lots of divisive political material.

And if you're looking for divisive subject matter—even for sketch comedy—you can't do much better than guns. Back in 2015 I produced a sketch titled "Burglars for Gun Control." Up until that point when it came to guns all I had seen on the sketch-comedy front was antigun propaganda masquerading (sometimes painfully) as comedy.

I'm sure you've seen these live-action cartoons before, where terms like "automatic" and "semi-automatic" are used interchangeably and gun nuts, in addition to being paranoid, reckless, and heartless, are always compensating for their tiny penises.

I guess in the case of armed women guns compensate for *no penis*. Have at it, ladies.

Have you ever thought about all the men out there who want to become gun owners, but just aren't ready to give up their big dicks?

But no matter how endowed you are, I imagine it is very hard to subdue a home intruder with just your cock. Even if you can do some wild stuff with it, like Sadhu rock lifts.

With this basically being the level of discourse in our ongoing national conversation on the right to bear arms, I thought, *Hey, what if maybe a gun could come in handy every now and then? What would that sketch look like?*

In the example of "Burglars for Gun Control," the sketch is about an armed young mother (recently widowed) who fends off two knife-wielding burglars who attempt to break into her home, while she is alone with her baby.

The twist is: I treat the thieves as victims of gun violence and the widow as a mad gunman. In the words of one of the burglars, "Her aim was way too good. I bet the gun was haunted by her dead husband!"

I was living in El Control de Armas, Los Angeles, at the time and casting for the sketch proved difficult. Originally I reached out to an actress I had known for years: great performer, wonderful person—she was perfect for the role. I sent her the script, but she couldn't tell whether the sketch was progun or antigun....Even with the title.

I know.

But I also thought that was kind of awesome. *See? Every now and then comedy can transcend party lines and ideology!*

But she made it clear to me that she was concerned about the "POV of the sketch."

In regard to the sketch's point of view, I told her how an actual event I had seen in the news inspired me to write it: a real widow, a real baby now fatherless, and two very real, violent knife-wielding burglars.

I explained how I thought my take on the subject would add some nuance to the discussion—or lack thereof.

But the actress made it very clear to me that what was important—in addition to the sketch itself, which she admitted was well-written—was my stance on guns.

To me it seemed crazy to think that "Before I can laugh with you, I have to agree with you." Or more to the point, "Before I can laugh with you, I have to make sure you agree with *me*."

Ultimately, she passed on the role and wished me luck—which felt like her sending me "thoughts and prayers."

I ran into this kind of casting trouble a number of times on both coasts. It's hard enough to write a script, cast it, shoot it, edit it, and get it to a place where you're comfortable sharing it with the world. Now on top of all that you're adding the extra stress of worrying about—what would you call it?—"off-type political casting?"

Will this progressive actor be comfortable pretending to mock progressives?

It's such a bummer on the creative level. Instead of opening more doors it closes them. And it leaves you wondering sometimes if the actor who turned you down now thinks you're a bad person.

Finally, I came to terms with this casting reality and decided, "Well, I'm comfortable with everything I'm producing. So I'll just step in front of the camera and do it myself when I need to."

Like gun ownership, casting yourself is another way to compensate for the size of your penis.

* * *

In spite of the sporadic casting woes, the thing I love about producing sketch comedy is that it gives me opportunities to work with writers, actors, and crew members I've known for years but maybe haven't talked to in a while. Some advice: People are always happier to reconnect when you're offering them money.

Years ago I was casting a project and floated the idea to my director of asking a certain actor if he would be in the sketch.

"Really?" my director said. "You wanna cast him?"

"Yeah," I said. "He'd be great. And we reconnected recently."

"But didn't you guys have a fight on Twitter?" he said.

So yeah—that's how we had reconnected. You don't talk to someone in years and then—BOOM—there they are in your notifications.

But my director's line of questioning really gave me pause. Because while the actor and I were going at it on Twitter—having a little squabble over the definition of "socialism," I stick to Marx's, while the actor was using a more colloquial version (think "who doesn't like being 'social'?)—I had totally forgotten that there was a real person behind the Twitter handle.

That person, I reminded myself, *the man behind the avatar* is incredibly talented. A great actor. And on top of that, he's someone who in real life I only had good experiences with. He was a champion of my work and helped me where he could. He had been nothing short of a great guy to me. The kind of person everyone would be better off having in his life.

And the idea that I would throw all that away, because we had a "fight on Twitter" really grossed me out.

It's crazy to think, but for many people that's how relationships go now. Arguments you would never have face-to-face are happening online. And because of one online dustup, your whole history with a friend or a colleague can be erased. Just think about it: there are people who cut family members out of their life over Donald Trump.

I don't know about you, but I don't want to live in that world. I especially don't want to create in that world. So, you're damn right I cast my old friend!

Too bad the video didn't do so well. I haven't worked with him since.

But didn't this story make you feel hopeful for the future?

* * *

Recently a couple long-time collaborators of mine asked that I credit them under aliases. They enjoyed getting the band back together and all, but they were concerned that if word got out that they were attached to my work it might derail future prospects for them.

It's not like the themes of the project were particularly controversial—but give it a few months and they very well might be.

My collaborators were apologetic, of course—and they did amazing work; the kind of work you would normally want the public to know that you did, but I understood where they were coming from.

They could have had more fun with their aliases though. I mean, if you're going to hide behind a fake name, really go for it.

I spoke to one of them at length—really, I listened more than I talked. It felt like I was hearing another confession.

They live with their family in the suburbs and have a BLM sign on their front lawn—just like the rest of their neighbors. They are doing everything they are supposed to do, as the good white allies that they are. And yet they still feel unease. After all, no Black people live in their neighborhood—even though it's official HOA policy that Black Lives Matter.

My collaborator and their spouse even discussed whether the BLM sign they have on public display is big enough. Keeping up with the Jones used to be about coveting your neighbor's Mercedes—now it's about coveting your neighbor's virtue signaling.

"Can you still see your house behind the sign?" I said.

"Yeah." They laughed.

"Then it's not big enough," I said. "And it will never be big enough. I'm sorry."

I've started to worry about the other collaborators, actors, and crew members I've hired over the years. I hope they're not judged by the sins of their producer. I pray, "May the only career I hurt be my own."

Don't get me wrong—I enjoy being controversial, but I don't want to be radioactive. Maybe I'm just compensating for something.

SHOW YOUR WORK

A fan reached out to me for advice on stand-up comedy. He was twenty-five, unemployed, and looking for "a little meaningfulness in life."

I told him I was a twenty-five-year-old aspiring comedian once. I'm forty now, unemployed (as I type this), and still aspiring.

If you're looking for a little meaningfulness in life, I said, start small, make the changes you can make right now, today. If you're unemployed, work wherever you can land a gig.

If you truly want to do comedy, always be writing and hit the mics whenever you can. "Open-micer" is often thrown around as a term of derision. And that's wrong. Open mics are where stand-up comics start—and even for working comedians they can be a resource to test material.

After six months of grinding, I told him, you might have five minutes of material you're proud of putting on tape and sharing with others. Share it, because you think it will give others a little meaningfulness.

If you approach creating with that intention, I bet you'll find just as much meaning for yourself too.

While the fan was asking about stand-up specifically, I think my advice works for all things comedy and even beyond. It's my little note to self.

I shared my advice on Facebook and got some wisdom back in the comments. (Something that rarely happens on the platform.) Matthew Tabor of *The Create Unknown* podcast wrote:

> There's an open mic parallel in virtually every sphere: something that on the surface seems low-level, but is critical to…not actually being low-level. Everyone who's serious about being excellent at something—or at least getting paid for it sustainably—recognizes that.

> Then the meaning part tends to take care of itself. The more you do, the more meaning surrounds you. You won't be able to help it. It will be everywhere.

> Plus, no one cares about what you think unless you've actually done stuff.

> So, do stuff. Don't limit yourself to reading about it or talking about it or weighing in on someone else doing it. Just do stuff, you zilch, and everything will get better.

Comedy is not a zero-sum game—even though it can feel that way sometimes. Over the years I've watched so many friends and peers become successful. But rather than allow indignation and bitterness to creep in—maybe just a *lil' jealousy*—I remind myself that there is no fixed pie. That if you want something to happen, it's on you to make it happen. By playing what you've got![63]

Over the years—starting with my college sketch troupe, the Wicked Wicked Hammerkatz, and then with my duo, Greg and Lou—I learned that I needed to take a do-it-yourself approach to comedy. I could never be at the mercy of other creatives. If I waited around for the perfect role to be written for me, chances are I wouldn't book it anyway. I blow at auditioning.

So, I cut out all the middle men and created characters for myself—the kind of representation that would never exist unless I brought it to life.

Who else but me is going to create the role of an eighty-year-old widower, Patch Whitewood, who makes a hat out of his deceased wife's pussy?

(Sometimes, kids, when you follow your dreams they lead to nightmares. It's a risk you have to take though.)

I started doing improv and sketch comedy twenty years ago—a couple years before YouTube came into the world. Today there are lots of videos of me floating around that I'm not happy with—the kinds where viewers leave comments like, "Quit comedy" or "Kill Yourself." I have to admit: sometimes my haters make valid points.

That's why to offset my shitty material, I make sure to have at least a few videos I'm happy with. It's much easier to convince people that you can be funny if you have evidence that you've actually been funny before.

Some artists though have such a sense of entitlement. They think the world owes them an audience and a paycheck.

---

63 One perk of reading to your kids at bedtime is that you may come across a line worth stealing. Read the poem "Ourchestra" by Shel Silverstein. The whole thing is worth taking.

If they have neither, it's because the system is holding them back. Both of those things may be true. Or you might suck. Show your work and let's find out.

Have you been hired solely to meet a quota? Same response: show your work. Because it has never been easier to prove you're talented, if you are.

Over the past two decades I have produced material that I'm proud of and my sketch comedy videos—some of my favorite work—have been viewed millions of times.

I even won a Webby Award. That's right—I am an award-winning writer and producer. You know, they call The Webbys "the Oscars of the Internet"—but no one believes that.

I take nostalgia trips down YouTube road, where hundreds of videos of mine live—original uploads, others ripped, some even dubbed over in other languages.

This little Greg-and-Lou ditty, "Wolverine's Claws Suck," has over 19.2 million views (and counting) on YouTube alone. Our goriest and most successful comedy sketch launched my career—but the video has been demonetized for years, and I don't even look like the actor who starred in it anymore. I'm not happy about the money Google is keeping us from earning through advertising, but I am happy to have transitioned away from that stage in life when I couldn't grow decent facial hair.[64]

The comments lately on the Wolverine video have been from viewers who first watched the sketch as kids and have returned over a decade later to rewatch what scared the shit out of them and made them laugh. The special effects still hold up—they're better than what you see in some of the X-Men sequels—thanks to the great Paul Rondeau who shot and edited our masterpiece.

---

64   As much fun as it would be to claim YouTube had it out for me because of my politics, it's just not true. We have other videos on the Greg and Lou channel that are still monetized and funny even after all these years.

Yeah, sometimes all this feels like success. It's also a reminder of how fortunate I am to be living and creating comedy in these amazing times. It is stupid-easy to get your stuff out there today. You have a studio on your phone. You have social media. You probably have a podcast.

I know, I know—everyone has a podcast! I have a podcast. (Subscribe to *The Lou Perez Podcast* and use promo code "LOU" for discounts on all your CBD and cold-brew needs.)

There is no longer one path in comedy—if there ever was one—which is scary but also liberating and something to celebrate. Comedians have more ways now to build an audience and make a living. If your work gives others a little meaningfulness, you'll know it. So aspire and show your work.

37

ODE TO THE UCB

Black people don't like improv comedy.

That is why so few do it or watch it. I know anytime there is racial inequity we are supposed to conclude that it is the result of racist policy, as MacArthur Foundation "genius" Dr. Ibram X. Kendi preaches. But in this case that is definitely not true. Improv is predominantly a white-people thing. And predominantly a goofy-white-people thing. There is no racist improv policy.

I know this, because I spent a great part of my life in the improv and sketch comedy scenes in both New York City and Los Angeles. In particular, at the Upright Citizens Brigade Theatre (UCB).

Improv gets a bad rap and rightfully so. There is a lot of bad improv. But when you see improv done well, it's magic. I don't mean it's like watching a magic show—there's a lot of bad magic too—I mean, it's like the people on stage are accessing the supernatural. And I remember that happening a lot on the UCB stage, whose house teams were made up of killers. What *National Lampoon* was to comedy in the '70s and '80s, the UCB was in the 2000s.

It was also an improv and sketch-comedy school. The problem with that is that the school started turning out people who figured that since they had spent all of that money on classes, they were owed spots on the stage. The reality though is that improv-accreditation alone doesn't make you funny. (Populate your program and programming with enough of those entitled assholes and your whole operation is bound to fail.)

Every year the theater would hold its Del Close improv marathon named after the creator of the long-form improvisation, The Harold, which the UCB four (Matt Besser, Amy Poehler, Ian Roberts, and Matt Walsh) brought from Chicago to New York and later to L.A.

If you don't like improv, imagine sitting through a non-stop weekend of it, where there is far more shit than magic. But also a lot of booze, drugs, and one year, I remember, Whippets.

I'm not sure if this was during the Whippets year, but I remember watching a late-night Del Close slot titled "Emanciprov"—where Black improvisers—I think all of them in existence—dressed up (down really) to portray American slaves.

The show's conceit was that their slave masters, a southern gentleman and plantation owner—played by an actor whose name I will not divulge—and his wife command their slaves to improvise as entertainment for them and their mostly white guests.

I, a free man, was part of that audience, packed into the theater space on West 26th street in Chelsea, in the basement below the Gristedes supermarket. Some of the pipes jutting out of the ceiling had black garbage bags taped to them to stop whatever liquid was in them from dripping on the stage.

I don't know what the one-word suggestion was that kicked it off, but the enslaved Black improvisers put on cartoonish slave accents and did *dey Massa's* bidding. I can't recall any individual scenes, but I do remember that the performance was so hard to watch that I had to leave the theater. I have no clue how it ended.

Days later, I spoke to one of the Black performers who had organized the bit. He knew me. I had been on a number of variety shows he hosted at the theater and normally I have a pretty strong stomach—but Emanciprov, that messed me up.

He laughed. He knew it was going to fuck people up and was happy to be partly responsible for that.

Emanciprov is one example of the crazy shit you would see on the UCB stage. Fearless stuff. (Depending on where you sat in the theater, your vision might be obstructed by the columns that were keeping the upstairs supermarket's cash registers and frozen-food sections from crashing down on us.)

Emanciprov also worked as a metaphor: to get most Black people to do improv you would have to force them to do it.

Over the years, the owners of the UCB, like good progressive allies did all they could to reach out to Blacks and other people of color with diversity scholarships and the like—but it was never enough to change the improv-loving demographic.

With Black Lives Matter protests inspiring activists to stand up to the supposedly racist gatekeepers of orchestras, museums, and the Poetry Foundation, it was only a matter of time before improv got the same treatment.

I couldn't believe the stuff I was reading about my old theater in publications like the *Los Angeles Times* ("Groundlings and Upright Citizens Brigade face racism and the 'comedy problem'") and the *New York Times* ("A New Improv Theater Tries to Be the Anti-U.C.B. Is That a Trap, Too?").

In the *L.A. Times* I learned about "the self-perpetuating white power structure fostered by these institutions [that] led to the belittling and marginalizing of diverse voices, racial bias in voting for team members, and lip service to the concept of inclusion while providing little mentorship or paths for advancement to Black, Indigenous or other people of color."

Maybe these motherfuckers just aren't funny? I thought.

And most of them aren't. But Colton Dunn, whom the *Times* quotes, is. He's a very talented performer, so it was surprising to read the following:

> Because of COVID-19, that capitalist hamster wheel has had to stop, and there's now time to breathe and realize what's going on, and to make changes," said "Superstore" actor Colton Dunn, who started working with UCB in New York City in 1999. He was one of the first teachers at the L.A. school in 2005, and he was one of three Black people out of dozens of performers. "So when UCB or Second City or the Groundlings reopen, how do we make sure they do so like phoenixes from the ashes of this old system that is infected with institutional racism?

It is always amazing to hear a successful actor decry capitalism. For better or worse, one of the fruits of capitalism is being able to pay hundreds of dollars for improv classes where you are almost guaranteed to never make any money with the skills you learn. The more improv you take, the less oppressed you are.

Also, I can't imagine allowing myself to be part of a "system that is infected with institutional racism" for over twenty years. Remember: It's an improv theater. You can leave anytime. You can even start your own theater.

Later in the article, Geoff Ross, whose work I'm not familiar with, asks, "'Is it wiser to try to get an existing organization to change and function the way you would like it to...or is it better to use your energy to carve out your own space?'"

Well, it's definitely harder to carve out your own space! According to his IMDb page, Geoff is only a year younger than I, so he should know. If there is an improv audience out there—say in Inglewood, instead of Hollywood—go get 'em.

I will warn you though, the Black rooms where I've performed stand-up in Inglewood aren't as forgiving as the mostly white spaces where BIPOC improvisers ask for a one-word suggestion to get the party started. You just can't guilt Black people into laughing.

I never heard about the improv revolutionaries at Project Rethink[65]—of which Colton Dunn is a founding member—ever offering to buy out the owners of the UCB. Of course, like building your own theater, coming up with the funds to make such a deal is difficult too.

No, what is easier is to weaponize your identity and use it to shame your white progressive allies into giving up what they worked decades to build.

Imagine how privileged your life must be if your way of dismantling systemic racism is to bring down an improv

65 The UCB's motto is "Don't Think." See what Project Rethink did there?

theater. I'm surprised I never saw a poster of Amy Poehler with her knee on George Floyd's neck!

The bullshit is so palpable in the following quote (emphasis mine):

> BIPOC performers must find and champion one another within the community in order to thrive, but mentorship can be lacking. Shaun Diston, who has been with UCB since 2008 and is one of the comedians behind Project Rethink, said *BIPOC performers must work five times as hard as other performers to get to the top.* Once there, they can get picked up for jobs in Hollywood and move on quickly. (Hollywood, he said, checks in now and again looking for BIPOC talent when it's trendy to do so.) *But the churn means that UCB regularly has a diversity gap, and promising students of color are sometimes moved up in the ranks before they are ready.*
>
> "After that well-intentioned move, they end up floundering because there's no support," Diston said. "They get spit out in a way that feels like, 'You don't value my diversity, you've used it, the joy has been crushed out of it.'"

So which is it: Do BIPOC performers have to work five times as hard, or are they moved up in the ranks before they're ready?

Don't expect this woke bullshit to make sense. Especially when it's being used to destroy art, livelihoods, and reputations.

* * *

I didn't realize how close I was to this story until I started writing this.

I began performing at the UCB my senior year of college, 2004. I didn't know anything about the theater, but the other members of my troupe, the Hammerkatz, were UCB fanatics. The prospect of performing on that stage—even without pay—was the ultimate.

Looking back, I can't believe how much time I spent at the theater—with the Hammerkatz and later my duo, Greg and Lou. On stage, both in live performance and midnight tech rehearsals. Not to mention rehearsing the sketches. And writing them. And rewriting them. And rewriting them....

I wish I had spent a lot more time there, performing and watching others perform under those leaking pipes.

Now at least one generation removed, I reached out to a former artistic director who was running things back in the day. In light of all the negative publicity in both print and in online grievance chatrooms, I wanted him to know how important he was in my development as a comedian, performer, and writer.

As the theater's artistic director he really made us earn our stage time. We all want our first drafts to go over well—and just get a run!—but as pissed-off as we might have been with the notes he gave, in the end he was right. He helped make our shows tighter and funnier and helped make me better.

Please do not take my sentimental outreach to him as a knock on his character. Or the characters of the truly talented performers who came out of the UCB.

I know I'm putting former members of the theater in a tough spot. Damn near all of them are progressives! But if posed the following question, how will they answer?

Was the UCB Theatre a racist institution?

If you say, "No," then you have to contradict your former BIPOC scene partners and the Project Rethink mission.

If you say, "Yes," then you are openly admitting that you were complicit in the oppression of BIPOC improvisers. You were just "yes-and'ing" systemic racism!

I don't expect anyone to answer that question.

All I can say is the UCB is no more and that is unfortunate. But, like so many performers and audience members, I was lucky to have been there—to witness the magic and even make some of my own.

38

LIVE, LAUGH, LOVE

'll leave you on this.

I want to tell you about my friend Keith, but I don't want this ending to be sentimental. Bear with me. My wife can give birth any day now, our house is still missing a kitchen, I haven't worked out in months, and everywhere I turn I'm seeing the words "Live, Laugh, Love."

My mother-in-law has a plaque hanging in her kitchen: "Live, Laugh, Love." The coffee shop down the block from where I've written a good chunk of this book has "Live, Laugh, Love" on a wooden block next to its La Marzocco espresso machine. Every day my wife and I are getting coupons sent to our new home address. If we want it, we can get up to 20 percent off any product with "Live, Laugh, Love" written on it.

Today the three words are reading less like that thing a middle-aged woman puts up when she's decorating her home because she needs something—*anything*—to take up space. No, the words are reading more like commandments.

"Hey, Lou. Live. Laugh. Love."

When my friend Keith died I was fortunate to get to attend his wake and funeral in person.

Earlier in the pandemic the mother of a friend of mine died from COVID-19. Alone in a hospital. No visitors allowed. An iPad with FaceTime her only medium of communication with her family on the outside. Her memorial service was conducted via Zoom. My wife and I attended it with a spotty Wi-Fi connection in our car—our son was there too, napping in his car seat.

We had escaped Brooklyn Heights to the outdoors of New Jersey and pulled into a parking lot to listen to my friend deliver a moving eulogy for his mother from a little box on the screen of my wife's iPhone. My friend was sitting on the couch in the living room of his apartment in Hell's Kitchen, dressed in a handsome black suit, his feet out of frame. I had no idea his mother had lived such a rich life or that my friend was such a good writer and storyteller.

I turned down the air conditioning in our car.

This is no way to live, I thought. *Or to die.*

* * *

Keith James Shaughnessy passed away two weeks before his forty-fifth birthday. I hadn't seen him in years. I didn't know he had a middle name. Growing up the joke was that Keith looked like a missing Baldwin brother. Not a brother like James Baldwin—but one of the Alec, Billy, Stephen, and Danny Baldwins.

In his casket, Keith no longer looked like a Baldwin. He didn't even look like Keith anymore. I think that made things a little easier for me. That wasn't my friend lying there, fully committed to this new role.

Instead of being buried, Keith chose to be cremated. I thought up a sketch—I can't stop the comedy bits from entering my head—where I hold a séance to reconnect with my friend, only to castigate him for committing the sin of cultural appropriation.

"Check your white bodily privilege, Keith!" I say, with lightning and thunder cracking around a spooky candlelit room. "It's time to decolonize cremation!"[66]

On my trip to Nepal years ago, I visited the *Basmeshowr Ghat* crematorium and watched the bodies of the dead burn in the open air. I remember breathing in some of their smoke.

Is it weird that I wish I had a chance to breathe in a little bit of Keith's? Just one hit, you know. Chase it with a beer.

I don't know where they spread Keith's ashes—doubtful they'll be gentrifying Nepal's Bagmati River, but who knows? Maybe with enough time. What I do know is that any water source would be lucky to have my boy's remains.

On the sidewalk outside the funeral home in Woodside, Queens, I joined the other mourners. I had grown up with these guys and years had gone by without seeing them.

"Check out Crimson Jihad,"[67] my old friend Walter says, pointing to my getup and my hair that's grown long under COVID-19.

I'm not even a minute in his presence—our friend lies dead in a casket inside—and I'm already getting goofed on.

"I thought I looked like one of the guys John Wick kills," I say, offering up some self-deprecation.

---

66   If only I had the budget to produce that video!
67   I had to look up the reference. It's the name of the terrorist group in *True Lies*, the Arnold Schwarzenegger flick.

Someone hands me a can of Budweiser. There's a box of them near the curb. Now more than a few of us are drinking on the sidewalk.

Keith was very generous with his time, his money, and his misadventures. Everyone has a Keith story, many of which—when you scratch the surface—reveal a lot of pain our friend was going through when he was alive. But somehow the stories are still hilarious. The types of stories that need to be told at your wake.

There we are sharing memories of our friend—in the convergence of life and death—when a woman walks past us and into the funeral home. We all stop to look. She is dressed in a low-cut, skintight, one-piece dress—even her mask is formfitting. While her dress might be black, it is more nightclub than wake attire.

I didn't know who she was. But she knows who she is.

The good thing about dying young is that there's a better chance a fine young woman will come to pay her respects dressed inappropriately for the occasion. It's the least you can do for your surviving friends.

* * *

Originally, I thought the author of "Live, Laugh, Love" was anonymous or a marketing guy for Bed Bath & Beyond. After about a minute of sleuthing online I found out that the three commandments are derived from the first three lines of a poem called "Success" by Bessie Anderson Stanley:

> He has achieved success
>
> who has lived well,
>
> laughed often, and loved much;

I'm not going to say "Live, Laugh, Love"—or the poem it comes from—isn't cheesy. But after all these years of doing comedy and finally taking the time to look back upon them, I realize that old Bessie is onto something.

All the intellectualizing of comedy—its relationship to politics, identity, and all the crap I've been going on and on about in this book—can get in the way of the profound simplicity of laughter and what it means.

If you're laughing that means you're alive. And there's no better time to be alive than now. And no better time to be making comedy than now. Again—it's not like I have a choice in the matter.

* * *

Keith died in November of 2020. I was fired from my job the month before. My son, whom Keith never got to meet, was born in March at the height of the pandemic. The hardest I laughed that year was at Keith's wake.

I realize that there is no way to laugh that hard without it hurting. And there is no way to make others laugh—like *really laugh*—without risking it hurting.

ACKNOWLEDGMENTS

I want to thank the following people for the laughs and the love.

My family: my parents, Luis and Florence; my brothers Sal, Marc, and Matt; my in-laws, Laura and Tom; Rob Miraglia; and my comedy husband for the past twenty years, Greg Burke.

My friends, collaborators, and co-conspirators: Jon Bander, Brandon Bassham, Yoav Bergner, Mark Boyadjian, the boys from Woodside, Dean Cameron, Fernando Castillo, Kira Davis, Jenny Diaz, Noam Dworman, Gene Epstein, AJ Ferrer, Hatem Gabr, Carla Gericke, Barry Goldsmith, Scott Hampton, Phil Hancock, Jessamyn Hope, Boris Khaykin, Mathew Klickstein, Gary Lee Mahmoud, Michael Malice, Chrissie Mayr, Barry McDonald, AJ Morales, Erin O'Connor, E. Gustavo Petersen, Anthony Raneri, Whitney Rice, Paul Rondeau, Todd Seavey, Larry Sharpe, Shelly Shenoy, Debra Soh, Ed Spangler, Sameer Suri, Scott Thompson, Harry Terjanian, Piotr Michael Walczuk, and The Wicked Wicked Hammerkatz.

Those who have supported me and my work: David S. Bernstein, Alistair Beaton, John Brodigan, Christian

Chavez, Jazmine Chavez, Andrew Conru, Echoes Under Sunset, Randy Epley, the Free State Project, FreedomFest, Jeff Mach, Mark Jay Mirsky, Fraser Myers, Brendan O'Neill, Lionel Shriver, Tom Slater, *The Spectator*, *Spiked*, Students for Liberty, James Taranto, Christian Toto, the *Wall Street Journal*, Young Americans for Liberty, and the Upright Citizens Brigade Theatre.

My wife, Michelle.

One night after dinner and drinks—and years before marriage and children—Michelle and I were walking along Brooklyn Bridge Park. She turned to me and after a giggle said, "Lou, am I your muse?"

Now if I were a painter or a sculptor you'd want to be my muse. But I'm a comedian. You don't want to be a comedian's muse.

But that reasoning hadn't crossed my mind at the time. In fact, I was quick to respond, "No, you're not my muse."

"I'm not?" she said.

"No. You're my rock."

Muses are easy to come by. But rocks are rare. When you find yours, well, you'll know what I mean.

ABOUT THE AUTHOR

Author photo by Paul Rondeau

Lou Perez was the Head Writer and Producer of the Webby Award–winning comedy channel *We the Internet TV*. In addition to producing sketch comedy, performing stand-up, and opinion writing, Lou also hosts *The Lou Perez Podcast*.

Lou began doing improv and sketch comedy as an undergrad at New York University, where he was part of the comedy group the *Wicked Wicked Hammerkatz*.

For years, Lou performed at the Upright Citizens Brigade Theatre in NYC and L.A., in sketch shows with the *Hammerkatz*, and his comedy duo, Greg and Lou. Lou was also a comedy producer on truTV's *Impractical Jokers*.